Kingdomtimekneelers@Hotmail.com

RUNNING TOWARDS THE KINGDOM

The Making of an Intercessor

THE INTERCESSOR

WestBow Press books may be ordered through booksellers or by contacting:

WestBow Press
A Division of Thomas Nelson & Zondervan
1663 Liberty Drive
Bloomington, IN 47403
www.westbowpress.com
1 (866) 928-1240

ISBN: 978-1-5127-2350-2 (sc)
ISBN: 978-1-5127-2351-9 (e)

Library of Congress Control Number: 2015920528

Print information available on the last page.

WestBow Press rev. date: 02/19/2016

CONTENTS

Introduction vii

Chapter 1 The Late 80's early 90's 1

Chapter 2 The Call 16

Chapter 3 True Wisdom can only be found in Christ 23

Chapter 4 The Purpose 38

Chapter 5 Only God can Nurture 44

Chapter 6 Free to Run 59

Chapter 7 The Power of Prayer-Uniqueness 68

Chapter 8 Finally Here 81

Chapter 9 Trouble is in my way. MOVE 87

Chapter 10 12-14-12 99

Chapter 11 Time to get back to the house of God 113

INTRODUCTION

The true Christ centered blessing surrounding the family of faith in God has been lost for quite a while. In my quest to find a better life, through reverent prayer and study of the scriptures I found it. Peace, Power, and Protection.

This book is about a member of the family of that faith, a member of the church of God in Christ Jesus. A member that left the faith and teachings of God and started losing in life horribly and almost lost it all, blindly thinking that he could continue to make it without God. That member eventually had to repent of his wicked ways and return to his faith, when things continued to fall apart and life no longer seemed worth living. That member is I, once a cast away of the faith, depressed, angry and afraid. I began living life recklessly and hopelessly and in despair, having nowhere to turn but God. Now rejuvenated in my faith by the mercies and goodness of God, all I can say is that I now found the true love of God and the Kingdom of God that Jesus spoke about in the bible, that kingdom is real and I found it in my heart of hearts.

Having found my treasure in Christ, I finally found that one thing in my life that has me grounded and committed me, to seeking God daily. I have a reason to pray and to fight for what I believe in, which is my faith in Christ Jesus. My new found faith in Christ equals eternal life and has given me a purpose to live and enjoy this beautiful earth. I almost lost my life to darkness and eternal damnation but now my days and nights are so full of life and worth living that I had to write a book. In the hopes of finding that person that could benefit from my testimony and appreciate the mercy and goodness of the Lord Jesus and my renewed strength in God. My mission is to win souls for God and to help teach and encourage my brothers and sisters to seek God's Kingdom of goodness no matter what you are going through. I firmly believe that we were not put on this earth to live in misery or defeat forever separated from God. Our heavenly Father has a purpose for our lives even in the midst of those dark lonely valley days.

I invite you as a friend, family member, brother or sister in Christ to take this journey with me as I share some of my valley experiences with you. Through my faith in Jesus and the scriptures of the bible, I have been able to renew my faith in God. I learned through painful faith trials how to live as an overcomer in Christ Jesus despite all of the errors, pain and suffering I once knew. I now know that God always had a plan for my life and I understand now how easy it could be to lose the playbook to the Kingdom of God with so much going on in life. It was really hard for me at times to understand my purpose but now I am committed to help share my testimony and success that I found in Christ. I am that brother of the faith, that rare breed of person, in this day and age which really does care for others success in our walk with God at every level, I care about people and I especially care for those that are looking for a better life in Christ.

It is not always peaches and cream, fun and entertainment following God's way during a true conversion. It takes discipline and sacrifice and most importantly, faith to stay on task at all times. What God has done with me and can do in you, also, is life changing and incredible. It is life changing, it is too good to keep quiet, and it has taught me that my faith in Christ is worth the fight and every battle I may have to encounter to receive Father God's blessing. I believe God is willing and able to change a person from the inside out if you believe and trust in Him. I don't care how separated from God you have been or how deep your sins may be or how much unbelief in God you may be facing at this moment. God is able to mend broken hearts. The God of Jesus Christ, Abraham, Isaac, and Jacob is no respecter of persons and if you are willing to change and have faith to change, than He is able to change you and bring you into His kingdom where you shall lack nothing because there is total peace to live life abundantly. I have had many ups and downs in my faith before this true conversion. There were times in my life where I thought I was winning only to find out somewhere down the road that I was wrong and needed to change in order to really win. The errors I committed almost caused me to lose my faith entirely because I was trying too hard to be someone else. I suffered greatly being double minded always trying to fit in with the crowd of faithlessness. God is faithful though and sought me through my confusion and has helped transform me every step of the way. His word (the bible) promises us that he has not given us the spirit of fear but of power, love and a sound mind. 2 Timothy 1:6

I have had many men and women of faith speak to me about the goodness of God but they never stayed long enough, for me to really find that good ground that God was about to give me. I believe that in the Lord's perfect will, it was meant for them to only be around for a short while. Well let me tell you, I have found that good ground and it is worth every tear you will shed to detach yourself from this world and set your eyes on heavenly things. There is a place, that the bible calls the Kingdom of God, Luke 17:21. I truly believe in my heart, that I have found that place, because I have given up everything that I used to love to do, in order to never lose where I am at in life. And let me tell you, I used to love to hangout and pass the time doing anything but read the word of God or pray.

Jesus Christ who is my Lord and Savior for his teaching and love sacrifice given to me and this world that believes in Him, spoke about his father's Kingdom in many parables throughout the bible. Jesus always claimed to be the true son of God sent down from heaven to share with the religious and lost sinners what pleased or displeased God. In fact, his first proclamation to the world was "repent for the Kingdom of Heaven is at hand". Matt. 4:17. How powerful is that, that even now over 2000 years since the crucifixion has passed men and women alike all over the world, can find and live in the Kingdom of Heaven that Jesus spoke about way back then.

In 2007 I found God's kingdom of heaven that was bringing me much healing, joy and peace. During this process of healing I began thinking about how I could share this overwhelming peace with my friends. All I could think about was encouraging others to pray and have faith. So one night at a prayer night service in my local church God gave me an idea so people could have something tangible in their hands to encourage them to pray. That tangible item is a very unique prayer pillow. In this book I will share with you my overwhelming sacrifice that I did for the Lord that took me through some very difficult valleys but through the goodness of God I continue to stand on solid ground with over 3000 prayer pillows all across the US and the world.

Since God's word comes alive in us daily I am just as excited about having you read this book as I am about writing it. Hoping I can leave an impression in your heart of the joy I feel to be called a Christian and a child of God. I pray that at the end of this book. You would be full of faith in God and encouraged enough to go out and run towards the Kingdom of God. With the confidence that God is on your side no matter what. Encouraged enough to never give up on your faith in Christ to pursue your dreams. It is a great joy to have you join me on this journey of trials, testimony and victory. I will be sharing with you some of my real life struggles but also the goodness of God to see me through them all, so buckle up, its time to keep it real and move forward in life by sharing the good news about the Kingdom of God and how God can take you from the pit to the palace.

CHAPTER 1

THE LATE 80'S EARLY 90'S

The late 1980's and early 1990's when I think of that time in my life, all I can is say wow! How the world has changed with all its technology. Who would have thought that the advancement of computers, cell phones and internet would have changed us all into such computer geeks? I say geek because in the 1980's while in high school that is what we used to call all the privileged students that took computer classes. There were very limited computers in schools back then when computers were nothing but a big electronic typewriter. The apple computer was nothing but a black tv screen with tiny white letters that really did nothing for you unless you were a writer. The floppy disc was the memory board. There was no color touch screens or graphic images at all. It all seemed so boring and corny with no real computer games other than some really low quality tennis game that was just a dot moving back and forth on your computer screen as you used the oversized spacebar on the keyboard to hit the black dot to your opponent's side. That game was more fun if you were able to afford the cost of the special controller needed to play it.

What a misfortune it was for me to not be accepted into that computer class while I was in school, instead I would pass by the doorway and make jokes or funny faces. Those fortunate students that got a computer seat assigned to them were on the cutting edge of technology for that time. I am sure that most of those young high school kids that were in that computer class are now grown adults with great computer jobs. Sorry for the computer geek jokes...I was only kidding.

In high school I was a bit of a prankster/jokester as most teenage kids are. I never considered myself to be a bully or tough guy in my teens. I was a polite respectful kid that got along well with everyone. I loved sports, going to school and working part time to make money after school. I lived with both my parents and 2 siblings in a small duplex in Bridgeport, CT. The neighborhood that I grew up in was not the greatest but it was not the worst either. We were a small family living on a tight budget living paycheck to paycheck as most people still do. I spent recreational time playing touch football or tennis ball baseball with my younger brother and friends on most evenings. That was one of our pass times that we did on our very narrow one way street that had cars parked on both sides of the street almost always filled with giant puddles of water on most curbs sides from the fire hydrant being used the day before to keep everyone from the block cool from the summer heat. We played many football games despite the puddles on that road and the unpatched street condition. The houses on that block were all close to one another with very little yards. The one way traffic that would often stop and interrupt our game of touch football seemed to never end with cars honking at us from time to time to get out of the way. We always speedily got out of the way of the car with the booming system, those were usually the cool teens or young drug dealers showing off their booming system. The parked cars were always a problem also when trying to catch the possible winning football pass that could win the street game of touch football. Sometimes we would crash bang into car doors, hoods or metal bumpers trying to catch the ball. Back in the day when you ran into a car, guess who got the dent? It was not the car, that was for sure. Cars were made with that military grade iron that I'm sure are still used on war tanks now a days and since I lived in what most people would call the hood, we had a lot of vehicles on our street from the seventies and early eighties that were made with that good sheet of metal. No matter how many times you ran into the car it was not going to get dented.

I had many fun days as a child growing up playing sports on our street, Butler Ave. in Bridgeport Connecticut was a popular for street games back then. We had many friends our age as neighbors and always would make new friends walking around the block.

The term bay bay's kids was street lingo for a family with a lot of children and it seemed like our street was full of bay bay's kids. The small one way street we lived on was often noisy with children playing and neighbors cranking up their stereos either from inside their houses or cars or parents just yelling out of their windows from the top of their lungs to get their kids attention to get home. Most children were either down the block or on someone's porch playing games. There were no cell phones or text messaging services at that time. Back then, to get a kid home for dinner you just needed some good lungs and a loud voice. Sometimes policemen would frequent our street because the neighbors could not get along with each other during the warmer months. Don't know what was in the air during the summer months but I do remember a lot of yelling and drama in which profanity was heard on a daily basis. A lot of the drama that was on that street was all about nothing, just families that wanted or needed attention. At the end of the day for the most part everyone got along. Even if it required a 24 hour lock up at the police station for some of the rowdy people that got out of hand from time to time.

Our family was the family that tried to mind our own business and just keep to ourselves. My parents were members of a small Spanish speaking Baptist church, which taught the word of God and believed in dancing in the spirit and speaking in tongues. So as a small child I remember seeing many people fall out in the spirit while attending church services. At times I got spooked by what I saw and other times I thought it was just funny. I never really understood what it meant to be slain in the spirit falling out. I was just a kid that went to church to make my mom feel happy and hang out with other kids that were forced to go to church also. All the kids I knew that went to church liked going to church because we had a gym with a basketball hoop in the church basement where most of us met up to play basketball. The children and young teens formed a common bond and for the most part we all got along.

I am the middle child of a family of 5 that attended church regularly. Father, mother, sister and brother, being the middle child was fun growing up but at times you could go unnoticed. As I became an older teen still in school and attending church regularly with my mom, I started to feel the messages and the testimonies of the people that attended church. I was not too serious about the things of God but I could definitely feel something was going on inside of me. One day, I remember getting prayed for by a pastor prophesying that I was going to be a pastor someday. To tell you the truth, I was not happy about that prayer because I did not want to be a pastor at 12. I did not think that pastors were socially cool at that age. The pastors I knew seemed like very serious men of God who instilled fear at times while preaching, I did not know the pastor that prayed for me personally other than what I saw from the pulpit. I do know some very down to earth cool pastors now but I didn't back then. I didn't think pastors were normal men or women that often go through the same issues most of us go through now a days.

As far as my feelings towards what that pastor prayed for me way back then. Well, my views have changed and now I would never reject that prayer. Pastors are blessed men of God often underestimated, underpaid and deal with a lot of community issues. I pray for them often now as an adult, that God himself would help them lead the flock and congregation of people that seek help from the church.

Life at 16 years of age for the most part was good. I have to say that I was a Sunday saint, going to church on Sundays and then during the week I would never really talk about God or seek spiritual guidance. I didn't do much seeking on my own either although I did read the bible on occasion and said small prayers from time to time, so I considered myself a Christian.

The music of the late 80's and 90's had a huge impact over my life. Hip hop rap music was the new stuff on the radio and I loved hip hop rap music. It was cool and now I also was radically cool. I had all the best of the best mix tapes in my room recorded right off the radio station onto a cassette tape. I wonder if anyone remembers that. When you could record right off the radio station with your boom box? That was cool, times sure have changed, bring back the cassette tape so I can record off the radio again, everything now is so advanced with most of the kids now playing video games and listening to music on Ipad's or handheld devices. Whatever happened to listening to the radio in your room with no TV or computer around? It was just you alone in the room with the radio blasting standing in front of a dirty faded mirror curling that straight bar with the plastic weights at the end, pumping up your bicep muscles. Or better yet how about squeezing that exercise thing that was like a car suspension shock that had hand handles at both ends and the resistance was some incredibly hard spring that was in the center and all you had to do was squeeze this thingamajig with both arms, till you made your pectoral muscles pop out. Man, those were the days, although bored yet never really bored because you knew that you were not alone, you knew that your friends across the street were all doing the same thing if not exercising they were practicing breakdancing moves listening to the Fat Boys beatbox. If you had a phone in your house back then it was a great privilege, if you had a cordless phone you were fancy almost high class material being able to speak to someone in the privacy of your own room without a cord. We couldn't affort to have the cordless at first but we did have a phone with a super long cord that was about 100 feet long, man you could walk to any room in the house or basement with that phone, my phone cord was so long that I could walk to the corner store and back, no problem. Untangling the cord was a nightmare, thank you Lord for cell phones.

The 90's what a great time in life for some, a true nightmare for others. The combination of being young and the way the music industry was changing from hip hop music to hardcore gangster rap was a huge turning point in my life. Drugs and gang violence was a growing plague in my city and it represented very well the growing gangster hip hop era. At ages 15, 16, 17 years old you were the perfect candidate for having your mind brainwashed to a good beat. I remember repeating vulgar songs that I now know invoked many evils, without even noticing what I was doing. At that time it was not a big deal we all could handle it supposedly but when drinking got involved surely nothing good would come out of it. Every day I remember getting deeper and deeper into the lyrics of a hard hearted walking dead man that made music and somehow got a record deal. I felt like I needed to listen to this music even though I knew it was hardcore and my parents would kill me if they heard me listening to such garbage. At that time I felt I needed to fit in because surely this was the music that all the cool kids and thugs were listening to and although I didn't want to be known as a thug. I had to deal with many wanna be gangsters daily so being of the same mentality was at least a benefit for me. We had many young thugs in my city and everyday, everywhere I went at least in my experience I always seemed to encounter young men that were totally thugged out. White, black, latino, asian, anyone with a black hoodie could have been characterized as a thug in the inner city even if you were a nice person deep down. As the hard hearted lyrics of gangster rap music pounded in my soul, I felt a sense of common ground even though I was not what I was listening to. The music would harden anyone if played continually and that is exactly what we as teens listened to, not realizing that a demon was hopping out of this lost man's gangster rapping and actually cursing those that listened it. Back then I did not know it was a demon but it was like clever cunningness by the enemy of God getting young people to be consumed by the evils that this music was producing. Not the beats or the actual rapping, it was the lyrics, the lyrics of devils. Lyrics that glorify killing, stealing, destroying and degrading women are not from God. Now I know that! But back then I just didn't care enough about the future consequences.. The Bible says that the thief comes to steal, kill and destroy. John 10:10. Those lyrics were deadly seed sown in the community and many young lives were ruined or even killed by its influence on the youth.

Unfortunately, I lost a lot of friends that I went to high school with or knew from around town to street violence. Bridgeport, CT was on the map as one of the murder capitals of this nation for such a small city. To a young thug, a city getting that type of recognition was like winning an Olympic medal (according to the FBI crime analst (lawstreetmedia.com)Connecticut still has 3 cities on the top ten list as the most violent 2013 report). My friends were hardcore and they gloried in it, my question was how could I this nice kid who attended church from time to time, hanging with the wrong crowd listening day and night to the wrong music about being hardcore, killing and stealing, not expect to get affected. I remember some really hardcore thug friends that I knew glorifying violence telling me to read the paper so they can show off who they shot. And sure enough the morning paper would read in the police log. "Shots fired. Masked gunman shoots 2". I would know about it in real time before the public knew. Not only that, but I also knew the masked gunman, little did I know that the devil was preparing me for a secret double life by keeping secrets due to fear. We knew better than to never let the police know. It was a sad reality for me to live with such dark secrets.

One night a friend named Rain that I knew from church but was not living like a Christian asked me to take a ride with him as we often did to go hang out and listen to music. He was a couple of years older than me so I looked up to him a lot for guidance and protection. We usually went to the mall to hang out or to the park to listen to music. This night was very different though. From the moment he picked me up his face looked cold and angry. A look that I knew all too well from growing up in the hood. The conversation was very short on what we were going to do that night as he stopped by another friends house to pick someone up. As I sat in the car clueless to why my friend seemed so angry. His friend that was sitting in the back was given instructions on where to drive. When we parked the car I heard the clicks of what sounded like guns being loaded in the back seat. Sure enough they were guns being loaded in the back seat. The young 17 year old sitting in the back seat was loading a 9mm handgun. He also had a stick that I thought was a baseball bat in the back seat, but in actuality that stick was really a sawed off rifle. The rifle had been cut down on both ends and then wrapping in bamboo wood to conceal it as a weapon. It looked like a baseball bat with a trigger. At that point I started asking questions like what was going on. The teen seated in the backseat started telling me how he was shot at by some neighborhood punks weeks earlier and how some of the pellets of a shotgun blast that he took had pierced his back. The kid in the back seat loading the gun was a strong muscular football player that was well known in high school for athletics. He was a very nice polite kid that liked to joke around alot but like alot of inner city kids that grew up in violent neighborhoods he could change that nice guy image into a violent almost unimaginable thug instantly. In the inner city it is almost like an animal instinct learning the game of survival to protect yourself. Especially if you have to walk the streets where drug dealers and gang criminals dwell. Well on this night he was going to get revenge on the guy that shot at him days earlier. He told me he was going to shoot the guy that shot at him if he found him, it all happened so quickly, I did not know what to say or do. Rain told me to drive his mom's car around the block and then to pick them up down the street near an abandoned house. I didn't know what to do so I just took the wheel and was down for whatever. I was 15 years old still barely legal to drive or have a license but in the inner city way of how I lived, I learned to drive by the time I was 14. With that said Rain gave me his mom's car and they exited the car with both guns. About 20 minutes later they arrive at the spot that they told me to meet them at. Thankfully no one got shot that night and everyone made it home safe.

Two weeks later, Rain picked me up again this time with tears in his eyes, to tell me that his friend, the teen that was with us nights earlier, did shoot and kill the guy they were looking for on that night I was with them. The high school athlete got the revenge he wanted as the man that had been bullying him began vandalizing his father's car in front of his house. Little did the man know or care that our friend was prepared to fight this time with his own gun. The man was shot within feet from where our friend lived. Shot dead with the same sawed off bamboo wrapped rifle that we were riding with the other night. It was very sad to hear that after he shot that man, he then went on his porch and sat down weeping for what he had just did. In such remorse he called the police himself to tell them what he had just done. Game time was over, reality just hit me that if the same outcome would have happened that night I was with them and someone would have gotten killed, I too would have probably been charged with murder. Sadly the young man that killed the other man was a well known football star that was still in high school and was about to get a sports scholarship to any college. He was a senior in high school and only 17 years old when he was sentenced to 60 years in prison as an adult, sadly this is what I lived out seeing day in and day out for the next 4 to 5 years while growing up in my city.

These pictures I took as a teen in my city Bridgeport, CT. in the 1990's Graffiti was used to memorialize those that lost their lives to street violence.

How do you break free from the pain of knowing young teen aged murderers or the one that just got murdered. Why did I have to live to see this side of life? Why couldn't I just go to school like any other high school student? Plan out my future and live a good clean life. You don't have to commit the crime in order to feel the pain the evil leaves behind. You get enough confession of real killers and you start to feel the same pain and misery they feel, you start to get that same cold look in your eye wondering if I am the next one to be on the hit list. I was too blind to see what was happening in front of me to see a real future without violence. I was trapped in the evils and I didn't even know it. At the time I thought it was cool, knowing hitmen and gangsters in my childish mentality. I looked up to them knowing that if I had a problem with anyone on the street, I knew many fearless trigger men that would glory in being able to shoot someone. Sadly, I befriended young teenage gangsters not realizing that I had become one too, they were ruthless in their violent crimes and many times did not get caught. Instead of running from them I entertained the thought of wanting to know what was on and in their minds to be able to shoot or rob someone with a sober mind. Instead of me sharing the very little light I had for God knowing that every relationship I had growing up seemed wrong, I said nothing. Don't know if it was because of fear or just restraint from the enemy over my lips. I did learn the excuse for thug life was all the same thing, young men trapped in a world of hate without God and without a hope for a better future. Worldliness, vain glory, anger, hate, all fueled by demonic hard core gangster rap music. I have had enough of this painful life God please set me free.

"Blessed is the man who walks not in the counsel of the ungodly, Nor sits in the seat of the scornful: But his delight is in the law of the Lord, And in His law he meditates day and night, He shall be planted by the rivers of water, that brings forth its fruit in its season, Whose leaf also shall not wither: And what ever he does shall prosper". Psalm 1: 1-3 (KJV)

I thank God for a praying mother and a father that always showed me a good example of being a family man and provider. They prayed for me and my friends often. I always remember my mother telling me to go to church and look for God. As a young man I was like ok yeah, yeah mom ok. I will, I will. But the day of seeking God and that true conversion was always so near but o so far. It was always far but near at the same time. I did attend church on some Sundays but I never got serious with my faith in God to live it out daily. I was the type of Christian that was very selective on who I spoke with about God and some times I was ashamed of my faith in God, the bible calls this mentality as being double minded. And I surely was double minded. But truth be told I was just weak in my faith. I was living a saint life to some and an all out worldly man to others, accepting the death of young people that I knew as too bad for them. Spilling some beer for my homies that did not make it and then...party on...sad but true. We grew up numb having to bury so many teens by the time we were in our twenties, that it no longer hurt to know about some young man's death. The pain and fear was so real that it just hardened our hearts towards all kinds of people, even the nice ones.

I gave up the gangster mentality and hardcore rap music for the party lifestyle realizing that those kids, those young killers that I looked up to for protection were now going to jail and the world just seemed to get darker and darker associating with them. Now all I wanted to do was exercise my right to party since I was fortunate enough to graduate from high school and was able to find a full time job rather quickly on my own. I had money in the bank and I had my own car. Hey, why not party? You only live once was my mentality. I made drinking alcohol and smoking weed a regular thing to do. In my ingnorance I never thought it would be a problem. The problem was and is that drinking is totally unhealthy and opening the doors to alcohol and street drugs being a juvenile was just like opening the doors to depression and being on an emotional roller coaster that never seems to end.

At that time I had a long time girlfriend that was still in high school that I cared about but getting involved with drinking and drugs was about to ruin that relationship. I was good at protecting her from the party lifestyle but I was getting lost more and more myself by trying to protect her. I found out sooner than expected that I was in love with the bottle and hanging out with my friends than I was with her. I knew that the way I abused alcohol was not healthy for anyone that really wanted an education and a good career in life. The pride of life and just wanting to be down with the world was tugging at me and I was too ignorant to look for sobriety or a proper education plan after high school. I wanted my girlfriend at the time to do well with her life but as for me I was too arrogant to see that the path I was on was going to take me on a long ride to nowhere. The cockiness came from the worldly attitude that I could handle life with drugs and alcohol and stop whenever I wanted to with no repercussions. So I let the hanging out time be with friends who also liked to drink and party. We were young and ignorant and on occasions we might have worked out in the gym to cleanse our sins but the real sin was being sown in the hearts and the attitude towards others that did not see life like us.

There was a time in my youth that I did enjoy working out and exercising to keep me fit. One of my favorite works out was playing basketball, running and lifting weights. It helped me get my mind straight after a night of partying. I hated feeling hung over yet week after week I continued to drink and party on weekends. Many times I would struggle to get out of bed let alone make it to the house of God. Thankfully I did make it to the house of God on some occasion to be cleansed from my sins but I struggled like most young people do in their late teens and twenties wanting to live life my own way without accepting counsel from my parents or spiritual leaders.

That was my lifestyle for a number of years until I stopped exercising or trying to be healthy because I was always too hungover to work out or just plain tired and unmotivated. In reality I was starting to lose what was keeping me partly happy, healthy and young. Which was faith in God and in exercise.

One too many times I let peer pressure and bad decisions keep me from prospering.

The bible says,

> "Do not be deceived, God is not mocked: for whatever a man sows, that shall he will also reap". Galations 6:7 (KJV)

CHAPTER 2

THE CALL

The call that forever changed my life came from my friend Rain whom I had not seen for years since his deployment to Iraq in 1991. Years earlier Rain had enlisted in the Marine Corp. to get away from the city in which we both grew up in that was ruined by so much violence mostly committed by teens or young adults. He was one of the first responders to the Desert Storm war. I was excited when I got the phone call because he was my best friend and I had not heard from him in such a long time. Rain was like my older brother having been raised together in the same church, we knew each other well, we played sports together, we fought together, we overcame the horrors of street violence together. I had nothing but love and respect for my brother. I was happy to hear that he was safe and doing well in Florida with his wife. I was even happier when he invited me to move down and live with him and his wife for a while rent free until I could get established so we could hang out once again. I was so excited that I had this opportunity to move to another state and start a new life with my best friend's support. It seemed like a no brainer, let me save up some money and in a few months we could start our lives as brothers once again. My life seemed like it was going nowhere in the city I was raised in and so I accepted his offer. I continued working the two jobs I had in CT in order to save up for this new life changing opportunity. At the time I was working two full time jobs, one was working from 6am to 2pm packing ice at an ice factory and the other was working 3pm to 11pm as a direct care worker/counselor for the mentally disabled population. I was working very long 16 hours days with the expectation of going down to Florida within a few months. I was doing my best to save all my money for the big move. I stayed out of trouble and stopped drinking.

A month and a half later I had about $1500.00 dollars saved up. I was very motivated and focused on saving as much money as possible. I knew that it would not be wise to relocate to another state without having a little nest egg of saving. However when God has a different plan for your life He allows things to happen to get your attention, sometimes we listen and seek after Him to help us make the right choice other times we blindly carry on and later suffer a worse consequence. Well I made the bad choice of not hearing God's warning sign because I ended up getting unjustly fired weeks before I was to relocate. The termination came to me as a thief in the night to destroy my future plans and rock my emotions. Instead of me seeking counsel from God, I let my emotions get the best of me and committed the biggest error of my life by leaving my home state totally unprepared with anger and hate, I left my home within the 24 hours of me losing my job. My termination was not justified in my eyes but through document manipulation I was targeted and let go. The manager that committed the fraud covered her tracks and blamed me for something that she clearly told me to do. My anger did not let me fight the good fight of faith to try to get my job back. In all probability I had a strong case to get my job back but instead I left to Florida the day I got terminated like a foolish angry man. I was so angry that this creep of a manager who was supposed to be my friend just ruined my plans of saving money so I can relocate in peace. I was desperate, upset and just wanted to get revenge. My past life experience associating with delinquents that loved violence was setting in. Certainly I was not going to go after anyone for no reason but now I had a reason and I was definitely angry enough to commit an act of violence toward the one that just harmed me. I was so angry that all I wanted to do was cause harm to this manager that had just lied on me and had caused me to lose my job. I was having a huge meltdown on the day I was terminated. In my anger I went straight home called in sick to my other job and started packing my bags. I feared that if I stayed around town any longer I was going to call some of my thug friends and do some real harm to this person that had just lied on me. It was better for me to go then stick around with all this rage I had. My mother did not know what to do when she came home from work and saw me packing my bags. She knew I was suppose to be at work. She was so scared for me because I was yelling at the injustice of me getting fired. All she knew to do to calm me down was tell me to please wait for my father to come home to at least say goodbye the proper way. But all I wanted to do was jump on the highway and go straight to Florida. I was so immature and should of handled myself better but now the lyrics of violent rap music was continually playing in my head. The lyrics that I had memorized from listening to corrupt music since my teenaged years. The music I listened to at the time was lethal to my soul it encouraged anger and violence, what a deadly combination at such a time as this.

Thankfully I did the right thing and waited for my father to get home. I was able to calm down some before I left on this life changing journey that night. My father knew my buddy Rain down in Florida and his family from church so I guess that is why he never really put up a fight for me not to leave. He just wanted to make sure, that I was sure I wanted to take this long trip alone, in which in my young mind I was. So I left that day to Florida but before I left I stopped to visit with a female friend that I worked with to say goodbye. This good friend refused to let me leave on my own to drive over 1500 miles. She was a good friend who really seemed to care for me. I call her a brave young lady for stepping in and showing more concern for me than the girlfriend I had at the time. My coworker showed me she cared for me in my time of need. All she wanted to do was be a friend and convince me to stay but she was also willing to take this road trip with me if she had to so I would not be alone. Her friendship was real and on short notice, since she could not convince me to stay she started making plans to take this road trip with me to make sure I at least arrived to Florida safe. It was less than 8hrs into my tragic day and here was this angel of the Lord planning to come with me to Florida to make sure I was safe. We left that night and drove for hours taking turns driving and drinking coffee to stay awake. It was a good road trip and I was able to get some of that anger that I had off my shoulders. I always felt bad for my friend that drove with me because I didn't receive her as the great girlfriend that she really was. I knew that she had all the qualities of a great woman but you never know what you have in a friendship until you lose it.

I arrived to the state of Florida within 24 hours after my termination. Happy to have made it safe I celebrated that night by going out with my buddy Rain and boy did we drink and have some good times that night. During this whole time I celebrated drinking and living it up for arriving at my destination safe. The one I really needed to be thanking was God for sending me an angel to accompany me on this trip. I hated the fact that I could not control my emotions on that day and now was prematurely in the state of Florida with anger in my heart. Leaving behind my naive girlfriend, my family that really cared for me and some good friends that were clueless to what was going on with me and what I had just done by taking off. We did not have any affordable cell phones in 1994 or text messaging to send out messages to anyone who was in your inner circle to let them know what was up with you. How young and foolish was I to run from my problems and let anger get the best of me. But what was done, was done and now I had to send back my lady friend that helped me drive down to Florida back to CT. Sadly I said my goodbyes at the airport and hoped to see her again someday. I never did though and we lost touch and I lost a very dear friend.

Now living in Florida with my friend for a few weeks. It didn't take long for me to realize that I needed to get my own apartment. Rain's wife was cool but I started to feel the pressure of it being time for me to get my own apartment. Rain would have never kicked me out of his apartment, his wife would have left before he sent me on my way. That is how close we were, we were brothers since childhood and he knew I was a go getter so he never had to worry about me not trying to stand on my own and move on. I had no desire to overstay my welcome and knew it was time for me to get my own apartment. So within a month I secured a full time and part time job. I was doing well enough on my own that I asked my girlfriend from CT to come down to Florida and live with me. She obliged and came down from CT to start a new life with me. Life seemed to be going great for me, I had my first apartment on my own and I was living with my high school sweetheart. I was working full time and part time and was starting to enjoy Florida. I was not rich but I was enjoying my life.

The problem that I was soon about to face was not knowing how to help someone that I wished I could help but couldn't. That person was my friend Rain. Not long after I got my own apartment, Rain was starting to struggle financially. His wife was pregnant and the stress he walked around with began to affect all of his close friends. Rain was always so angry that after serving his country, he could not find a good paying job to support his family. I always wished that I could of done more for him since he always seemed to look out for me. I just did not have the solution to his problems. I did what I could to help him out but I really was in no position to solve all the problems he was having financially, emotionally and spiritually.

Employers sometimes forget to honor the men and women that serve this country. Some employers are so demanding that they lack understanding when hiring a young vet that has come back from war. Rain certainly had some issues that could have been resolved if he knew where to get help as a young non injured veteran. At the time I did not know how to help him other than to encouraged him to not give up. I hated seeing my friend struggle having to see things go from bad to worse. He did not deserve to lose his job nor have to scrape from the bottom of the barrel after having served his country. Just as Rain recieved his last paycheck from a job that never paid him enough, his only means of his transportation began to give him issues. His car would break down over and over again. When his family could not help him I would step in and transport him to fill job application. I loaned him money to get his car fixed but as soon as the problem was fixed some other auto issue would come up until he had to finally junk his car and be without transportation for a while. Like a good friend I transported Rain here and there to fill out job applications but it was hard on me working two jobs to make time for him at times. Instead we would hangout after I got out of work.

When life decides to throw some curve balls, man they sure do come hard and fast. During hard times if anger and depression set in sometimes you can make some bad decisions that will sink you even more in the hole or you can begin to pray and make some faith based decision trusting God to make a way out for you. In the next chapter of my life I will illustrate a perfect example of how the blind leading the blind can cause so much pain and despair that both shall surely fall in the ditch.

Matthew 15:14

14 Let them alone: they be blind leaders of the blind. And if the blind lead the blind, both shall fall into the ditch. (KJV)

CHAPTER 3

TRUE WISDOM CAN ONLY BE FOUND IN CHRIST

As my friend continued to struggle, I enrolled in college for a short time while living in the sunshine state. I had no real focus on what classes I was going to take. I just remember signing up for a class because that is what everyone else at my age was supposed to do. How could I know where I was headed if smoking weed and drinking was my new pastime. I really didn't want to go to college for an education, I just wanted to meet other young people to celebrate life and connect with young people in school that really just wanted to party. Who cares about getting an education when by the age of 21 you feel like you know it all? Besides I was young and sooner or later I was going to grow up before all the real tough times in life came my way, right? Nah, I was so wrong! Life holds back no punches at keeping you oppressed and keeping your mind stuck in the ghetto. Life has no timeline to follow, it just reproduces either good or bad fruit. In this world system there are two groups of people, you are either a winner or a loser and what defines winners and losers to a people that does not have God in their lives is money! If you have money you could deceive the world into thinking you are a complete success, a well rounded individual that contributes and cares for the needs of others but really do not. I found in my new saved life that true success is found in a person who is willing and able to make leaders out of followers. Success is being able to have time to attend the needs of others. Success is about being a light to this world that is suffering and sharing of your time and knowledge to help others reach their destiny. You don't have to be wealthy to give your time and encouragement to help others move forward. You just have to be a willing vessel, a light for God.

The road that left me to much suffering was found along the path to living as the world lives, chasing money and the wicked pride of life. Money made me either extremely happy or extremely sad to have it or to not have enough of it. I was always a money maker since my childhood. So the roots of me knowing what money could do for someone to be a little bit happier always ran deep. As a teen I would cut grass, shovel snow, work odd jobs around the neighbors house to get paid. At 15 years old barely of legal working age, I worked full time at a fast food chain working double shifts on weekends. I would do whatever it took to make or have money. Making money and working all the time instead of getting an education at fifteen years old blinded me to the fact that I needed to properly plan for my future education if I really wanted to be successful some day as opposed to just having cash. I always felt like "the man" in high school who was going to be successful in sales because I always had money and knew how to talk with people. I started my career as a salesman in school selling m&m candies to pay for things like my prom tickets that were very expensive at the time. I sold so many candies in the first few weeks that the money I made from candy sales paid for two prom tickets ($70 each in 1991 that was expensive back then), prom photos and my prom tux. I often would sell out of candies so much so that my friends would ask me if I could sell their candies for them. At that time my popularity for selling m&m candies allowed me to sell my friends candies for them, I sold out often. That was just the type of teen I was, I cared and so I shared in my success as a candy salesman even if the money was not for me.

In the hopes of finding a better life I moved to Florida but without proper planning I ended up living a nightmare haunted by the demons of my past and future present. My faithless attitude kept me surrounded with faithless people and the darkness that surrounded those that didn't have an active relationship with God became my stumbling ground. My crew was mostly friends that I grew up with in CT now living in FL. We all knew and understood each other well. Even though we were all a little rough around the edges we all tried our best to be nice and friendly to everyone. We were all looking for a better life at our young age down south. Trying to escape the streets that had left so many of our friends dead or in jail. Living in Florida gave us that opportunity to start fresh but without an education or the fear of God in our lives, we were doomed to fail. We were friendly but had harden characters that came from growing up in the inner city. None of us could predict the future pain that would destroy our friendship forever. God knew it but we just wouldn't give Him the time of day.

I was never the type of person like I had mentioned earlier to be violent or unjustly angry at anyone yet I would still listen to negative music and hung around people that had no goals or vision for a better future. In the 1990's I was witness to many ruthless thugs selling drugs openly on street corners. Shoot outs, fights, long prison sentences and eventually murder was just a way of life in my city or at least that is the way I saw it. You were one of the lucky ones if you didn't get caught up in some sort of violence or crime as a teen. I hated people that would rob others. I had been a victim of a real violent attack one time as I skipped class in high school to go get me a sandwich at the corner store. I was mugged at 11:30 am across the street from my high school of all my jewelry and kicked in the face for resisting my robber's demand of opening my fisted hands so he could steal my gold ring as I lay on the pavement in broad daylight in the parking lot of a small convenient store within feet of my school. I had an imaginary line that I didn't cross and robbing or strong arming people was just wrong. Being a victim of a violent crime had it's impact on how I developed as a young man and the hardening of my heart.

Getting back to my buddy's situation things just seemed to get worse for him. All he did was complain about not having enough of this or enough of that and it was starting to get on my nerves but I didn't know what else to say. I tried my best to advise him to not give up on looking for a good job but with no running vehicle how could he find a job in Florida if everything seemed to be 30 minutes or more away driving.

As for myself I dropped out of community college and began working as a ticket agent to all the major theme parks in the central Florida area. I was perfect for the job because I was very outgoing and despite all I had been through in life I maintained a happy go lucky attitude. An attitude that tourist could appreciate, I was very friendly. I liked my job and I was looking forward to selling timeshare real estate one day because that was where the real money was at. But my night life of always wanting to party in Florida was not letting me flourish. I was trapped and committed to my boys from back north who were now my neighbors again. Although I was trying to be a leader by working full and part time I started to realize that part of my friend's problem was that he was not trying hard enough to better himself and had no faith or real ambition to do better, all he looked forward to was another night of drinking and talking about how bad his situation was. All the while I was picking up the tab. One night as we were drinking listening to some gangster rap music and smoking weed he suggested to me that I should let him rob my ticket booth where I did business from so he could get caught up on his bills. He knew I was in charge of selling tickets to tourist attractions that could be worth thousands in the black market. At first I said, "No, you are not going to get me involved in this nonsense". But he was persistent insisting on knowing the layout of how my company ran its business and with all the weed we smoked, listening to rap songs that glorified robberies and killing, my mind began working in the favor of the evil that was lurking in the air. The evil one the bible states comes to steal, kill and destroy, the evil one is a spirit sent by the devil. John 10:10 (KJV).

The enemy of truth and justice was at work on my mind with seeds of corruption planted everywhere. I wanting more by working less, listening to corrupt music that encouraged evil and taking intoxicants that numbed my decision making. It was only a matter of time before the poison fruit of committing a crime was evident. Day after day I was absorbing my friend's negativity by hearing how bad his work situation, money situation, and how he was starting to hate his wife. Since I did not have any other friends that lived near me I tried to pass the time by entertaining my friend, bringing him to bars to play pool really just trying to make his day a little better, trying really hard to clear the air. I felt bad for him so I picked up the tab everywhere we went. Little did I know, that what I was doing by spoiling him would do more harm to us both and then to my own financial situation, relationship with my girl and my own health mind, body, and soul. I believe one of the hardest things to do in life especially for a true conversion is let go of friends that you know since childhood but sometimes it is necessary, to let people go.

I don't remember exactly how or when I gave my friend the information he wanted about my ticket selling operation. All I know is that within a few weeks we were planning to rob a hotel of its ticket selling concession stand. He wanted me to play the victim but I refused, I already had so much guilt for giving him the information. I would rather he did his dirt while I was not there. He made a promise that no one would get hurt if I gave him the information he wanted. He promised and I believed him. I know deep in his heart he did not want to commit any crimes to get paid but times were getting very hard on him and he convinced himself that committing a crime was the only way. I did not know who was going to be on shift the day the robbery was to occur. I really did not know any of my coworkers. Since I floated to many different locations I did not know everyone who worked for the company. I had many sleepless nights knowing that someday soon a major crime was about to be committed. By then I was so lost smoking pot daily and drinking, that the enemy had won and I did not care about truth or justice and the concerns of those that I would soon hurt. The price of the crime was definitely not going to be worth the financial reward. I was a sinner and I needed Jesus desperately.

23 For the wages of sin is death; but the gift of God is eternal life through Jesus Christ our Lord.

Roman 6:23 (KJV)

On the day of the robbery I remember getting that 6am phone call to come pick my friend. I told him to forget it, I did not want to have any involvement but he was not taking no for an answer. He persisted that we should go forward because his partner named Chopps who was his brother in law, was also ready and waiting for me to pick them both up. He complained once again about not having the rent money and that he needed to do something before he was to be put out in the streets. So with the fear of God running through my bones I left my apartment early that morning to go pick him and Chopps up. My job was to drop them off and pick them back up at the location down the street, just like when we were 15 years old kids living in CT, looking to shoot that guy that was messing with my friend's family. Except this time the mission was definitely going to get done and I was now going to be part of an armed robbery. Even though I did not see anything or have any contact at all with the victim, the criminal justice system would see my part in this crime because of the information I had given my friends, and for failing to call the authorities knowing that a crime was about to go down.

The robbery went down as planned without anyone getting injured. We got away with the crime for a short time celebrating our victory but things were soon about to change. After weeks of partying in the club, spending cash on clothes, drugs and women, we were in our minds the new mafia boys on the block. The darkness of committing the crime on that day was fresh on our minds almost daily and starting to give us an appetite for more. Once sin has entered the heart and there is no remorse. You better watch out because now the stakes just got higher and the enemy that you just opened the door to is seeking for more wickedness to fill his ego. Regardless of who gets hurt in the process.

In the weeks that followed, I was robbed at gunpoint in my home by my so called friend, the brother of Chopps. This dude named Shady, who was a heartless criminal who would rob his own friends if he had too. And although I considered him a friend from up north, he thought it would be a good idea to blackmail and rob me for the crime his brothers just committed. He believed that I benefited greatly from the robbery and he wanted money just like everyone else so he targeted someone that he thought he could get over on. I don't know how he assumed that I was the mastermind but that is exactly what I was made out to be. Shady was the brother in law to my best friend Rain. As much as I don't like to admit my involvement I have to take responsibility for what I could have prevented. I should have stopped the crime before it ever manifested, by saying no, I will not be part your crazy idea to get quick cash, I know now I was being targeted with a purpose. If God was to truly set me free one day from all of my sins. I had to accept my involvement and repent for the harm I had just done to another person even though I was not at the actual crime scene. I was about to reap what I sowed without me knowing it and karma was about to have her way on me.

Shady who had visited me at my apartment on other occasions one day showed up uninvited to my apartment. He and Chopps rung my door bell and asked to come in because they had some very private stuff to talk about. So I let them both in and brought them to my bedroom so we could talk. My girlfriend at the time was in the living room watching TV. Shady started talking to me about some officers that were in his neighborhood that questioned him about the crime that we did. He said that they had information that he was involved and that it was only going to be a matter of time before they returned with a warrant. I found his story to be a bit insane but he said that the officer had given him his business card threatening to arrest him soon. Since I didn't really believe him I said, let me see the card. He said, ok I have to get it because it was in his car. So he left to go to his car to get the business card. Chopps stayed with me in my bedroom shaking his head not knowing what his brother was talking about and appeared to be worried. Minutes later Shady arrived back to my room with something wrapped in a towel. As I let him in the bedroom I saw that what was wrapped in a towel was a sawed off shotgun, immediately his brother Chopps ran into my bedroom's bathroom frantic. Shady shouted, that we were now going to do things his way and demanded money from me. He had a sawed off shotgun pointed about three feet from my chest. I am like, what is going on because Chopps had run to the bathroom yelling at his brother to stop doing what he was doing. I on the other hand was just so confused and trying to figure out if Chopps knew his brother was there to rob me. Amazingly I was the calmest I had ever been but fuming with anger on the inside for what was happening in my bedroom as my girlfriend was in the other room watching a movie clueless to what was going on in the room next door. Shady kept demanding I give him money or he was going to shoot me. I said shoot me then because I don't have anything to give you. Realizing that I was not scared of him or his threats towards me with a gun pointed to my chest.

Next, he said with the most demonic voice, I smell money in this room and if you don't give me some money I am going to shoot your girlfriend. To me that was the turning point of me breaking or holding out to his demands because my girlfriend did not deserve to get shot while innocently watching TV in the other room not knowing what was going on in the bedroom. So I immediately backed down, when he said he was going to kill or shoot my innocent girlfriend. In order to get him out of my apartment, I remembered that I had hid a thousand dollars in the kitchen. So I told him to let me go to the kitchen where I had hid some cash. He agreed to let me out of my room to go get the cash. I went to the kitchen got the money and handed it to him. I was livid consumed with anger for this supposed friend now pointing a gun at me and robbing me in my own house. I knew that I had to get him out of my house before I snapped so after he got the cash, he and his brother that was hiding in the bathroom left. Amazingly they both apologized to me. Shady said," sorry but I have to eat too". I said," don't worry about it no problem", just get away from my apartment was my concern. I could not believe the violation that I had just went through. I was fuming, I didn't know what to do! The guy that just robbed me was suppose to be my friend and more importantly he was the brother in law to my best friend. He had me between a rock and a hard spot because I knew that if I called the cops he would blackmail me and tell the cops about my involvement in the robbery that had just occurred weeks earlier.

The next day I held a meeting at my best friends house in which Chopps attended, yeah the guy that was hiding in the bathroom while I was being robbed by his brother. Chopps swore that he had no idea his brother was going to rob me that night. I believed him so I pleaded with them to do something because this was their brother who had just robbed me at gunpoint and was blackmailing me at the same time. I expressed my anger and feelings of betrayal to the one who just violated me. Too my surprise they said sorry, this is between you and Shady. I was so angry at their response, so once again I reminded them that it was not me who robbed the hotel it was them and if they were to get caught for the crime it was going to be because of Shady. I just wanted to resolve the issues I had with Shady with them backing me up but again, they washed their hands and said that the problem was between me and Shady. I remember storming out of my friend house telling them I was going to kill Shady, just to see if I could get a reaction from them both. Their response again was hey do what you gotta do. I said it again, "I am going to kill your brother", making it very clear that I was not joking this time and it was the same reaction from them, do what you gotta do. I said, "ok, its my own problem you are right, just stay away from him." So I stormed out of the house and went about my business, planning to get at a pistol at a local pawn shop early the next morning. The damage to our friendship was done. I grew up in an instant! "What have I been doing hanging around these two losers, nothing good!" It was too late!

I could not believe how my life was majorly ruined overnight. First I leave the state of CT with the thought that I was going to kill my manager, fleeing to another state in the hopes of finding peace and reuniting with a friend and brother that I loved dearly. Only to get wrapped up in a world that was much worse than the one I had been living in a year earlier in my own home state. The robbery and the lust to get money by any means necessary was because I was looking out for a friend. I had a job I was not looking to make a quick buck that way. I just wanted a new life and to share it with a friend that I thought cared about me but it was apparent that he didn't and I fell into this pity party trap for him that, now had got me in a major jam. I was no longer a 15 year old kid but I was still following behind a childhood friendship that I felt I owed something to because we grew up in the same church!

What a terrible situation I allowed myself to get into, as if I owed my friend anything for defending me a few times in my youth. Wow, What a mess! I was now in a living nightmare with the fate of others in my hands. I had a major decision to make and it was tormenting me because the death angel sitting on my shoulder with a bull horn over my ear telling me you must avenge this scum of a friend that just robbed you. He must die, he is going to get you locked up, he must die! I was now facing the demons of my past calling me to murder. Being reminded of all the youthful murder confessions that I had heard over the years reminding, me about why they killed. Now I finally understood the anger, I understood the pain and the feeling for revenge. I debated over and over on what should be my next move. I was looking for mercy for Shady but I could not find it. I was looking for grace for Shady but I could not find it. I was so far away from God that I could not even remember a scripture to save my life, let alone the life of another man that just violated mine.

To my surprise in just a blinking of an eye I had just realized to the full extent the evil person I had become by believing all of the lies the devil so cleverly planted in me. With all this anger inside I could feel the devil asking me to commit murder. All the confessions those young thugs made to me as a teenager was coming back, I could feel the devil telling me it was my turn, it was my time to kill in order to get my next promotion. I was so lost and confused desperately looking for that gun that would seal my fate. I had to kill this dude that robbed me in my own house. What type of man lets that type of situation go? No man! So as planned, I went to a pawn shop to get a gun that morning. Luckily a new state law had just passed weeks earlier that you had to wait 2 weeks and pass a criminal background check before you could purchase a firearm. I remember the anger and anxiety clearly, I also remember being fed up with all the evil that I was doing to myself. I remember being in the parking lot of the pawn shop that I had just filled out all the paper work to get a gun. The memories of my youth came over me, the good and the bad times. A flash of the many funerals I had attended as a youth burying another young soul came over me and I just began crying out unto the Lord asking him for mercy, remembering my friend that had killed someone when he was 17 and being sentenced to prison for 60 years. I pleaded with God that I did not want to hurt let alone kill anyone. To become a murderer was not the reason I relocated to Florida, I did not want to be known as a murderer. I didn't want to be known as a thief either but this is what I was becoming. I didn't want to live in fear being on the run either just in case I thought I could get away with murder. But it was very hard for me to let go of what just happened to me a few nights earlier. What I had just been living was a lie and at the core I still believed in a good God. The embarassment and the shame I felt in a flash overwhelmed me. So I began bargaining with God telling him that I rather pay for my involvement in the robbery than commit murder. I plead with God for mercy on me. I promised I would change if God was merciful to me and would take this pain and misery away. I didn't know what to do but I could hear God promising me mercy. I knew that I was not going to be able to shake off the anxiety without the help from the Lord. So after praying and crying out for help, I did as I felt instructed from the Lord.

Weeks earlier I had been in communication with an army recruiter. I was trying to get away before the crime went down. I was on a waiting list to enlist in the military before the crime came to fruitation but that never happened. This time I went down to the army recruiting station and told my potential recruiter what had just happen to me, seeking his advice. Jokingly he told me he had an arsenal of weapons and some friends that could help me out. As I explained to him the seriousness of what was really going on in my life he did advice me to call the police and make a complaint, he said he would go to court with me and testify how I had been waiting on the formal test dates to enlist. So with that testimony I made the decision to trust in this soldiers advice. Even though I had known Shady was going to blackmail me and his own brothers it was the right thing to do. I had made up in my mind that it was going to be better that I suffer for a season even in prison than to suffer in prison for a lifetime for murder. It was a real intense moment for me and I knew I had to do this or else I was going to commit some more serious damage to my own soul from all the pain and torment that I had already been feeling. As much as I knew it was going to hurt to end up possibly in jail, I trusted that the Lord had a plan for my life, always hoping for mercy from the courts.

So later on that day I rented a uhaul truck and packed my stuff ready to take a road trip back up north, I quickly explained to my girlfriend that I was bringing her back home to CT. Because my life and her life was now in danger and that there was a 50/50 chance that I was going to be locked up.

My girlfriend at the time was scared but understood as I laid out my confession. She promised to be with me no matter what. It was heart breaking to say the least to ruin someone else's life after she had found a job and was in school planning her education, but I figured that if I got her home she would be safe and able to start over, this time alongside her family. Minutes after the truck was packed and I was ready to go back to CT I went down to the police station and made a formal complaint. I just wanted this man that was now my ex-friend to pay the price for betraying me. For hurting me so much, this dude was suppose to be my friend and he visited me regularly and there was no reason for him to have come in my apartment rob me and then threaten to shoot me and my girlfriend. My revenge was going to cost me my life as a Floridian as I knew it. It would cost me friendships and brotherhood loyalty that dated back to my childhood years but in my heart my friends abandoned me and stabbed me in the back at one of my lowest points in my life. The stress and fear of my fate was soon to be in the justice system and that alone weighed on me more than I thought I could bare, but at least I was not going to go to prison for murder. It didn't take long before we were all arrested and a man hunt was put out for me. By that time, I had already left the state of Florida not realizing I had a warrant for my arrest and my picture was being plastered all around TV screens in the central florida district. All I was trying to do was get my girlfriend back home safely to CT.

CHAPTER 4

THE PURPOSE

I titled this chapter the purpose because God had a plan bigger than I could imagine. God had a purpose so great for my life that as I sit here writing of his purpose, I think back to how about if I had not trusted God on that day 17 years ago, where would I be? Every decision I made in my life from that day forth would be forever recorded in the book of life as a decision to suffer for the cross to get my life right. It really was a faith based decision up held by a praying mother, up held by that minister that prayed for me when I was a child prophesying to me. Little did I know that the beginning of true trials in my faith were going to be tested, it would be a rough roller coaster ride that the enemy would try to control. The enemy had no plans on making my life easy by turning to God for help and exposing how easy someone with good intention could get lost in a world of complete corruption. I just wished there could have been a better way. There was no way out now and the reality of my sinful nature was about to break me and humble me like never before.

> 24 O wretched man that I am! who shall deliver me from the body of this death?

25 I thank God through Jesus Christ our Lord. Romans 7:24-25

The day that I feared came quicker than I expected. I was arrested less than 72 hours after I made that police report of Shady robbing me. Luckily I had made it back home to Connecticut. Unloaded my furniture and brought my girlfriend back home to her mother's house. I had enough time to give my father my possession for safe keeping and explain to him my situation. I let him know that there was a 50/50 chance that I would be arrested. Always hopeful that the police would not believe whatever that jerk would eventually tell them. It would be all lies because I never robbed anyone. It was his brother and brother in law that did the actual crime. He would have to give them up too and since they never wanted to help me, well I had to do what I had to do. If my friends that had committed the crime got arrested on the grounds of what their own brother tells the police, well, then I could live with that, because when I went to them for help and those jokers washed their hands of everything and would have let me go down for murder if I would have killed their brother for robbing and blackmailing me at gun point.

The night of my arrest would happen as I was returning the Uhaul truck to a return station in CT. I remember it being a little after 5 in the evening. I had a friend follow me in his car to the Uhaul return site. As I was driving the empty truck with no wallet or ID on me. The only piece of article I was carrying was the police detectives business card with a case number on it from the complaint I had made before I left the state of Florida. On route to the Uhaul center as I waited for the traffic light to change so I could enter the highway, from behind and in front of me comes an army of police cars, some undercover in unmarked patrol cars. Sirens blasting, police lights flashing everywhere and cops in plain clothes and in uniform with their guns drawn surrounded the uhaul truck, yelling driver get out of the truck. I immediately put the truck in park as 2 police cruiser were now in front of me blocking my path from moving forward. I had no choice but to put my hands up and say ok you got me. When the officers pulled me out of the truck they yelled at me what is your name! I responded with my brothers name. Not more than a second later I saw one of the officers had a clear picture of me with my name written on the bottom and immediately I said that's me and then stated my real name. Good thing I did that because, I would have caught another charge for lying to police and misrepresentation. Amazingly I was not one bit scared, I would have thought that I would have been more frightened by all this commotion knowing I was going to jail but I wasn't. I knew that the game was over and there was no way I was getting out of custody. My heart was either hardened or I really just trusted God I don't quite remember. The arresting officer was the high school patrol officer that monitored the high school grounds I attended and the officer that took the police report when I got mugged across the street from my high school way back then. The officer was in total shock because he remember me instantly. He said, what happened to you? The last I remember of you was that you were a victim of a robbery. With the list of charges on the warrant that included armed robbery I assured him it was all a misunderstanding and showed him the police business card I had from Florida PD. He was so shocked because he remembered clearly how violently I had been attacked and robbed that day in high school. He must have remembered the swollen bloody eye I had from being kicked in the face while I was a teen. He was very polite to me and wished me the best of luck as he booked me at the police precinct. He even shook my hand and wished me the best as I was lead away to a jail house cell. I saw the Lord's hand in my affairs from that point on because the police officer was very kind and he was very sincere when he wished me the best. God bless him for his kindness and for remembering me from high school that I was a good person.

With a bond of one hundred and seventy-five thousand dollars I could not make bail. I would spend a month in a Connecticut jail before the state marshal from Florida came and extradited me. The time I did in CT jail was rough 23 hour lockdown with no recreation time. You only came out of your cell to shower and eat, it was one of the worst places you could ever want to be. I had no roomate to talk to so I spent a lot of time comforting myself by praying to God and singing any church song that I could remember from my youth to comfort me as I wept silently awaiting my day in court. The day the marshals came and got me was horrible. I was shackled with chains attached to my arms and legs. I remember not being able to see much because I did not have my seeing glasses and I am as blind as a bat without them. Next, I was transported in a dark paddy wagon to a small passenger airplane. It probably held ten people max. That night I went on a flight plan road trip with the marshals because I could hear them talking about picking up two more prisoners in Pennsylvania, and sure enough when we landed it was not Florida but Pennsylvania I spent the night in some other state, in their jail until morning totally clueless to where I was.

The next day when we finally made it to Florida I was so numb to all pain. Being transported as a prisoner from one state to another has to be one of the most humiliating adventures that I had ever been on. I was hungry, tired and about to move into a new prison home with my co-defendants eagerly awaiting my arrival. I tell you this trial was only the beginning of a long nightmare that seemed to never end. When you decide to get your life in order, it is then you realize the gravity and consequences to your sin. But God is faithful in not giving us more than we can bare. I still to this day don't know how I survived those lonely nights without tightening a rope to my neck and killing myself. I had no one in my corner. I had no family in Florida to visit and comfort me. My friends in the south were now my enemies and I was about to ride out a jail sentence all by myself in a state that was miles away from my family. What did I get myself into?

When I arrived to the Florida jail where my co-defendants were I was eagerly waiting to run into one of them if not both. I had to see who was the rat that got me involved in getting charged with 6 felonies. My charges included robbery, armed robbery, burglary dwelling, carjacking, false imprisonment and grand theft. What a mess and what a hefty lengthy prison sentence I was looking at. I could not believe it. I was nowhere near the crime, I did not even see what happened let alone carjack anyone but that is exactly what I was facing. It is a scary thing to come into the criminal justice system with a list of charges so great that any one of them was sure to get me 15 years in prison or more. Some of these prosecutors just don't care and will try you with all they have to try and get you a life sentence in jail with no mercy.

God knows the truth though and it was in Him who I trusted in. So no matter what I was charged with, I knew that God was going to make a way. I had to trust him no matter what.

About a week later I was put in the same cell block that my co-defendants were in. To my surprise they both came to me and welcomed me to the cell block where they had made it their home for the last month and a half. When I arrived another prisoner who I did not know came to me saying so you are the mastermind huh, at that point Rain my co-defendant came to me and we exchanged the paper work that had the list of charges and statements. Both Rain and Chopps saw that I had made no statement against them. Yet when I saw their paper work my best friend Rain, the ex-military man had made me out to be the mastermind of the crime. Wow! That was a major blow to my case and faith in any type of friendship, I was so angry that this dude that I was trying to help since day one would throw me under the bus so violently. It was he who did not have the job. It was he who was always complaining, It was he that did not have a car, It was he that asked me for the layout of my business and it was he that would not take no for an answer on the day of the robbery. Yet he made me out to be the bad guy. I was so upset that I requested to be transferred to another cell block. The only cell block that was open was a pod called the nurture cell it was a Christian based cell block, where you had to follow rules and regulations. In this cell block, prisoners had to make up their bed bunks every morning and stay awake and attend bible classes. At that moment I didn't care about how I had to do my time as long as I was away from these guys that have destroyed my life. So I left the regular population pod and was headed to the nurture center cell block with an eager mindset to really learn about God and get my life and mind in order.

CHAPTER 5

ONLY GOD CAN NURTURE

Overweight, depressed and feeling hopeless I arrived at the nurture cell to be greeted by some prisoners that you can clearly tell were different. I felt comfortable immediately and knew that this was definitely a more pleasant atmosphere to do my time. The cell block I left was like a small zoo compared to this library like cell block that I had just transferred to. I was not yet a hardened prisoner so I got along well with everyone and I had no problem following the simple rules of the nurture cell like, no fighting, no profanity and making your bunk every morning. Along with no sleeping during the day while bible study was being held. Not a problem, I looked forward to the challenge and more importantly to changing who I was. I needed God desperately and now I had a chance to know him in a peaceful atmosphere. It would not be long before I dedicated my life to the Lord, through a preaching that a guest speaker would bring forth. He spoke about the resurrection power of our Lord and Savior Jesus Christ and what salvation is, he also spoke about forgiveness of sins, and how God heals broken hearts daily.This faithful servant of God week after week would preach and teach faith in God through Christ Jesus. He also was a musician so he would bring in his keyboard and would sing with us, pray with us and teach us from the bible, how many great men failed God's commandments often but God still used them. He taught me that true grace and mercy is only found in God the father. God is an awsome wonder. This faithfilled minister always brought the joy of the Lord to every meeting. The joy and peace was infectious. I never felt like a prisoner when fellowshipping. I started to feel connected to God in a way that I had never felt before.

It reminded me of the peace that I felt as a youth when going to church. When I knew no sin. The peace of God I felt day in and day out while doing my time, was real. I knew God was working on me so I would wake up early and stay up late reading the bible and learning about God, I didn't feel like sleeping my time away. Instead I started getting into a routine of praying, reading the bible and working out.

At the time of my incarceration, I had been about 50pounds overweight from all the smoking and drinking I used to do and eating junk food all the times. In the nurture cell I started losing weight rapidly by getting up early saying my prayers and walking. I would do laps walking around for hours in the small living corridors that I had now made my home. I must have walked for miles. I would sing songs of deliverance unto the Lord and when it was time for every prisoner to be locked up behind bars for the evening. I would stand in front of the locked cell and jog in place. Within a month I must have lost 20 pounds from all the walking I did and from the days that I would fast meals unto the Lord. I was a prisoner in the natural sense but my soul was set free through my faith in Christ. I clearly remember the day the Lord sent a guest speaker that would come forth with a powerful word from God about speaking in tongues and receiving the Holy Spirit. The preacher on that day spoke about the day of Pentecost found in the bible in the book of Acts the second chapter, titled the day that God made good on his promise. The preacher had emphasized that if we were all on one accord that day during the service, that God would do the same miracle he did with the discipiles in the bible story. He reassured us that even though we were in jail and being punished for our sins, paying our debt to society that God loved us and wanted us to be blessed. He stated that when God forgives and saves a man it is at that point in their faith towards Jesus that the forgiveness and healing begins, being in jail did not hinder the Lords blessing to us who believed in Him. We all believed the preacher that night.

My faith in the things of the Lord was getting strong and I certainly wanted all the blessings that I could get while they were available, so I placed all the faith I had in God that night we had service, expecting to receive the gift of speaking in tongues and the power of the Holy Spirit. As the preacher man finished up the sermon all the men were standing in a circle holding hands. It certainly felt like we were all on one accord that night. The preacher began praying mightily for us to receive the Spirit of God and speak in new tongues. As the preacher walked around our circle he would pray for us and then tap us and immediately the Lord's Spirit had most, if not all men speaking in tongues out loud that night. It was a glorious night to be recorded in heaven.

What the gift of tongues did for me that night was make me more sensitive to the things of the Spirit of the loving, merciful, infinite God. I still did not understand the gift of tongues but I was definitely a changed person. I had the peace of God in my life so much so that fellowshipping with other prisoners changed, I now considered them my brothers in Christ. I had not known my fellow prisoners crimes or why they were in jail nor did I care to know what they had done to get them to where they were at, that was between them and God. What I did know was that things were going in the right direction for those prisoners that sought the Lord.

Weeks after that prayer night service, I continued to pray in tongues. Not much at first but a little bit at a time in private on my knees when I was alone in my cell. I started to have more hope God was still in control of my case and the truth getting out, so I could come home soon to my family. I was not yet vindicated or sentenced I was simply doing time, not knowing my fate. I spent many nights praying and asking God to forgive me for my involvement. I was angry with the devil for deceiving me and making me a criminal. I knew that I was not the bandit and this criminal mastermind that the state of Florida was making me out to be. I come from a godly home and my purpose to move to Florida, was to make a better life for myself alongside my best friend but somehow we got caught up in a very messy situation.

My mission now that I was incarcerated and committed to my Christian faith was to change as a person, earn my freedom and learn to fight these evil spirits from within these prison walls that had put me there. I often questioned myself. Why did a young man like me end up in prison? Why did I have to go through this hardship if all I wanted to do was start a new life near my close childhood friend? So I continued to pray and looked for God in everything I did. I could no longer trust anyone but God and His word. I clung unto God with everything I had. Some nights were better than others no matter how much faith I had in God doing time was very hard. My cure for those real depressing nights was to exercise to elevate my spirits. I had to make myself well from the inside out. If what I had on the inside was anything good, surely it would have to shine through on the outside. That is exactly what I did and I spent many nights just focused on prayer and exercise. The peaceful place I found within these prison walls during my alone time gave me much hope. I felt great and like a brand new person, I knew in my heart that if I could find this secret place of peace that I had just found inside these prison walls on the outside that I could accomplish anything I wanted in life, I just needed to get home to begin my new life with Christ as free man.

It wouldn't be much longer before my case would be presented before a judge to accept a plea bargain. God seemed to be working on my behalf and I was starting to look forward to going home soon. As my sixth month of incarceration neared I get a dear john letter from my girlfriend. It was very painful to know that the person you have been with for 5 years has decided to move on. It was hurtful but I had nothing to offer, I didn't even know when I was coming home. Many of the men I was incarcerated with had suffered much pain at the hands of losing their spouses or girlfriends. They encouraged me to just stay focused on my faith in God and when I got home that the Lord would provide the perfect woman to help me get back on my feet. I wept for my teenage sweetheart but I had to let her go and trust that God would not abandon me. I still had to get out of this place before I could handle any women affairs anyway. This was my time to get right with God and move forward in the hope of being released soon.

Psalm 25

25"Unto thee, O Lord, do I lift up my soul.[2] O my God, I trust in thee: let me not be ashamed, let not mine enemies triumph over me". (KJV)

Well the day of sentencing was approaching, my faith was strong in the Lord and I was ready to take responsibility for my mistakes. On the 8 month of my incarceration I was sentenced to one year in the county jail with the time that I had done thus far as credit, so I had 4 months left. Praise the Lord! God had done a miracle because anyone of those charges could have gotten me up to life in jail. I was very thankful but sad at the same time because I would from that day forward be known as a convicted felon. As much as I urged my attorney to get that record adjudicated it did not happen and I did fear for my future employers asking that question of me being a felon. What would I answer? At least I was going home soon and I had a release date and for that I was very thankful. I called my family in CT and I let them know the good news. They also were very thankful for God's mercy and grace towards me. I couldn't wait to be with my family again.

After sentencing I was asked by the chaplain of the nurture cell program to move back to regular population with the other inmates that were not part of the Christian program. They needed my cell and bunk to make way for new inmates that were on a waiting list to get into the nurture cell. I agreed and the next morning I was to be moved into the zoo life style of doing time in regular population again. I call the other cell block a zoo because it was loud and noisy, cussing and fighting among inmates was the normal and there were no rules to follow. I didn't know what to expect now that I was a changed person going back to reality of prison life, being locked away with the hardened hearts of thugs and murders who didn't care anything about God or my conversion. I had faith that God was with me protecting me and would keep me safe. I was now fit doing 500 pushups and 500 situps a day running in place for miles plus I was 50 pounds leaner. I was not worried. On the day of my transfer I was blessed to have moved into a cell with a believer of the faith. This new roommate was an older gentleman that passed the time singing songs to himself and talking a lot about life. He was cool with me and we got along well. It would not be long before he realized how committed to my faith I was. I was mostly quiet and didn't talk bad or bad mouth anyone, I stayed on the same disciple routine that I had practiced for months in the nurture cell. I prayed, read the bible and would read anything positive and worked out daily.

It would be about a week into my transfer to a new cell block before I would be tested by someone who was not impressed with me. The incident came as I was going to get some ice out of a cooler that all the prisoners used to drink from that was locked up in a small cage. The cooler held ice tea and was locked inside a cage that was easy to move because the cage was larger than the cooler. The cooler was like the ones used at pro football games, the only thing was this one was empty, no drink only ice at the bottom.

The only way to get a drink to cool my parched mouth was to get the ice from the bottom of the cooler. By unscrewing the top of the cooler you could get to the ice that was in the bottom of that empty cooler. Well I did that and one of the other prisoners that was a very scary looking strong brother jumped up out at me from his nearby seat where he had been playing cards with some other big guys and yelled at me, "leave that alone" and then came to stop me in front of everyone. It was very disrespectful and definitely a moment that he tried to seize to intimidate me and get respect from everyone else. I played my hand cool knowing that I only had 3 months left in my sentence before I got a chance at freedom, and I was not going to let anyone or anything get me in trouble. It was a trial of my faith to see if I could control my own anger by having someone that did not know me yell at me like I was his child. I was upset with this guy coming out of nowhere to yell at me. I had just finished working out and I was thirsty and at least wanted some ice. So I simply walked away and let him enjoy his moment with his homeboys all laughing. About an hour later while I was in my cell reading the word, the inmate that had just tried to punk me came to me and apologized. I was so shocked. He was a man that did not look like he had an apologetic bone in him. I would later find out that he was a man of the Muslim faith and as rough and tough as this dude was on the outer shell he was cool with me and we became friends. We shared in our belief and faith towards God with each other and learned about some of our differences and some of our likenesses in our faith towards God. I was encouraged by his courage to come apologize to me. He did not have to do that but God had a purpose. From that day forward I began being friendly with the other inmates, I would come out of my cell and talk with everyone. I would share my faith with whoever gave me an ear to hear.

Within days I would be having bible study in my cell room with a few of the other prisoners. The bible study would grow and we would move from cell to cell having bible study in each other's living corridors. I remember in our bible study services that we would have no music or musical instruments to play so we would make beats by hitting the side of the metal toilet bowl to make a drum beats, it often sounded really good and you could feel God was really moving amongst the cell blocks because prisoners were getting set free. Due to the faith of a small group of believers and the commitment to keep having bible study, the zoo like atmosphere was changing and the word of God was now being studied on a regular basis in small groups. The entire cell pod was beginning to be a quieter place to do time, it was not the nurture cell but it was definitely quieter and more peaceful during the day than when I first arrived.

At night a group of us were having some very powerful prayer night services that could be heard by everyone right before the lights went out. It was just a few of us at first but I remember that every night about fifteen minutes before lock up the guards would flash the lights on and off to give us a warning that we would have to wrap it up soon. Well that warning light became a huge blessing, because as soon as the lights would flash a bunch of us, would make the call to prayer time by clapping our hands and shouting prayer time trying to encourage others prisoners to get out of there bunks and come to the main pod to join us in prayer. Incredibly a few weeks after transferring from the nurture cell, God began moving in the hearts of all men that were in that pod. I will never forget the first night that the prayer circle grew so much that God had gathered all the men that were living in that pod to make a giant circle to pray holding hands in the center of the main housing unit.

There was no help from outside ministers in this cell or the prison guards to keep the peace. It was just a bunch of men that believed God for mercy and were now seeking him through prayer. Wow, that was incredible! All sorts of people with all different cases some of murder, some of robbery, some of drugs all holding hands seeking God's forgiveness and peace through prayer.

All praises to our father God who received all the glory for the two or three of us that had faith and courage to encourage prayer in the midst of such faithlessness. I could imagine the guards looking down from behind the mirrored glass tower praying with us also. The circle grew and prayer continued every night. Every night someone different would lead the prayer group and I was more than blessed and honored to lead such a large group of men in prayer from time to time, the cell pod where I was housed was home to about 50 or more men. Praise the Lord God almighty for showing his goodness to all men. Praise the Lord God because when I entered that pod it was a zoo, there was no prayer time before lights out but now I was part of a movement that gathered men to pray and seek mercy and grace from father God. And it was not just a one night affair, it was a movement that continued until I was released. What I had learned in the nurture cell I was now teaching and being a light to other prisoners in another area of the prison giving men of all races and different faiths hope in Jesus. What an awesome God we serve. I even remember my friend who was a faithful praying Muslim man with us on the night before he was to go to court. The anointing of the Father was so strong in our prayer night services that even my friend had faith that night to come pray with us Christians. I was overjoyed to see him in our prayer circle because I had asked him several times to come join our prayer circle but he did not because Muslim men usually have their own time of day and custom to pray but, God himself moved on this man's heart and the next day, when he went to court, all the charges were dropped and he was released. Praise God for his mercy unto all men.

Psalm 107:1-2

King James Version (KJV)

107 "O give thanks unto the Lord, for he is good: for his mercy endureth for ever.

> 2 Let the redeemed of the Lord say so, whom he hath redeemed from the hand of the enemy";

With less than a month left on my sentence I started to get a bit comfortable with the people I was doing time with. I started playing the game of chess more frequently and was winning most of the time. There was an older new inmate in my cell pod that was some sort of chess champion that drew a large crowd of inmates around the table every time he played. This guy was the best of the best and liked to play the speed round version of chess. I also liked playing speed chess. I was good at it and I considered myself highly skilled at checkmating my opponent with any piece. Well even though I was good I was not considered a champion like this other guy. There was no doubt that this gentleman and I were going to face off one day. Well that day happened with a series of three back to back games on a day that one of his friends had gotten beat by me in a chess game. Like a little kid this mutual friend was trash talking me for beating him and he wanted me to play the older guy who was the champ. So as a bunch of inmates gathered around the table to see if we would finally face off, I took the empty seat and set up the pieces. I remember it being a very quick game less than a minute and in a few moves I had checkmated the old man. Everyone was shocked, I was even shocked that I had beaten this guy so quick. So without thinking about it we switched color pieces and setup the game again. This time he went first and within a few moves I had checkmated this guy for a second time. The inmates surrounding the table made so much noise that night that I am sure the guards overlooking from the tower were ready to rush the pod as they watched us play. As the place got louder and louder with lots of trash talking amongst the other inmates as to who was going to win the last game. It seems that I made some believers of me that night after winning back to back games against their champion. With in minutes my supporters began placing food bets on the 3rd and final game. So we set up the pieces for the third and final time, this time I would go first again.

The game was slowed down a little bit but in the end I still came out victorious. I had just shocked everyone that had bet on the old man to win. He was very upset that night because he was a gambling man and had just lost his morning breakfast on betting that game. I am sure he was cursing me as I celebrated my victory silently. He was not the nicest of people (sore loser) and in the excitement of the game we did not have prayer that night as a group before lights out.

I am writing about this game time victory because little did I know that the enemy of my soul was using this time of play to get me out of focus with my prayer life and study time. I was losing ground in my faith without me even knowing it, to celebrate being called a chess champion. I was now more interested in staying up playing chess betting on myself to win than prayer. Forgetting that God had a greater purpose in my life for me to be in that cell pod than to play games and now my defenses were down and in a matter of time the enemy would strike a blow to injure me and rock my faith towards God.

Ephesians 6:10-13(KJV)

The Armor of God

10 Finally, my brethren, be strong in the Lord, and in the power of his might.

11 Put on the whole armour of God, that ye may be able to stand against the wiles of the devil.

> 12 For we wrestle not against flesh and blood, but against principalities, against powers, against the rulers of the darkness of this world, against spiritual wickedness in high places.
>
> 13 Wherefore take unto you the whole armour of God, that ye may be able to withstand in the evil day, and having done all, to stand.

One early morning about 8am as I lay asleep in my cell on my top bunk bed, I was awakened to what I could only describe as a painful nightmare that I soon came to realize was real. It was not a bad dream, what I was encountering and going through was real and a very frightening experience that would scar me for a very long time. What happened to me that morning was that I was being assaulted by another inmate with a heavy duty mop ringer. As I lay asleep, all I felt was someone yelling profanities and hitting me as hard as they could over my head with this high school cafeteria style mop ringer. I was wacked three times with so much force that the heavy duty plastic of the mop ringer handle broke. All I could do at the moment was yell out in fear and pain for what I was going through. Once I realized what was happening to me I jumping off my bed to grab my attacker. I could not see clearly who it was that was attacking me. I did not have my glasses on and I was very blind and dazed in that moment. All I could do was grab and run the person that was attacking me into the jail house bars and hold onto the rails trapping him in with my body, until the guards came into my cell to break us up. It happened so quick but the trauma of going through that nightmare definitely did some damage to me both physically and spiritually. I was angry with God for allowing me to get assaulted. The person that assaulted me was my co-defendant

Chopps, who had found out that I was to be going home soon and decided to transfer to my pod to attack me and basically tried to kill me in my sleep. I had not heard or seen him in about 10 months and the devil used him to attack me that morning being that I had just 2 weeks left on my sentence.

That violent attack tested my faith in Gods protecting power. I was so angry at God that I didn't want to pray anymore especially with the other prisoners. I was angry at my cell mate that was doing time with me in that cell block who betrayed me by leading this attacker to my cell without waking me up or defending me. I was angry because everyone that lived in that cell pod knew that I was a man of God, how could they betray me and not wake me up before I got attacked. These unanswered questions left me with a heartache and emptiness that haunted me for years after my release. Little did I know that God was still in control and no matter how angry I was, God had a plan and purpose for allowing me to go through that attack. It would be years before I could understand why God would let me go through such an attack. I could never say that God was not with me protecting me through that attack. The force that I was hit with while I was sleeping that day should have caused brain damage or worse killed me. It was an angel of the Lord blocking the force of impact over my head that kept me alive. I now thank the Lord for sending down his protection in the midst of my attack, it could have been so much worse.

From that point on I no longer prayed in the prayer circle with the inmates, I knew the person who betrayed me and he was a Judas in my eyes and I refused to get close to anyone. I only had a few days left before I would taste freedom. So I kept to myself once again, no more chess games. I just focused on staying out of trouble.

On the day of my release Nov. 12th 1996, I could finally say I paid my debt to society. I was a free man with my parents at my side ready to escort me back to Connecticut. What a joyous day, fifty pounds lighter and stronger in mind, body and soul. All I wanted to do was eat some real comfort food, some real Italian pizza, some real burgers and fries and drink some real coffee with lots of sugar and cream. I was truly grateful for the opened door and the things that I learned during these very difficult times. I am still thankful to the Lord for opening that door to freedom and the new opportunities that I find in him daily.

Psalm 48 (KJV)

King James Version

48 "Great is the Lord, and greatly to be praised in the city of our God, in the mountain of his holiness.[2] Beautiful for situation, the joy of the whole earth, is mount Zion, on the sides of the north, the city of the great King". Amen

CHAPTER 6

FREE TO RUN

Excited to be back in Connecticut I contacted some of my childhood friends to let them know about my conversion while I was away. Most of my friends had not known about my incarceration and wanted to know what went so horribly wrong. As much as I wanted to minister to them I really did not know how to, it seemed like so much had changed. I was settling in and getting back on my feet was all I wanted to do. Making a better life was all I wanted to do but I didn't know how to fit in anymore. I felt all I had in life was my faith in God, with a will to do good, a felony conviction, and no clear direction on how to overcome this next chapter in my life. It was good seeing some of my old friends and spending time with them but it was obvious that they did not have the inward solution to staying connected to the God I had met months earlier. They just wanted to comfort me by taking me out to have a drink and talk about anything but God. I tried to share my new faith in God with them but it always felt inappropiate especially when I started to drink. Ministering to friends and getting back on my feet as a free man was a lot harder than I had expected. I was soon losing my discipline to study God's word and pray as I had done so many times before. I had been through some real tough times. A major life changing event that involved some very deep emotional pain, I needed to stay rooted and grounded in God's word, if I was to survive. I was a wounded soul wandering in the wilderness just trying to start over again. Over time I lost my discipline to pray and study or put into practice God's word.That would cost me my health and peace and an endless cycle to start over and over again searching for the Lord as if I did not know my redemeer lived. As happy and strong that I looked on the outside, I was now realizing how deep a wounded vessel I really was.

> "But when Jesus heard *that*, he said unto them, They that be whole need not a physician, but they that are sick". Matthew 9:12 (KJV)

You would have thought that the hardest times I spent in life were the nights I spent behind prison walls for committing a crime. But I tell you the truth the hardest time in my life was spent after my release. The hardest time was coming home and trying to figure out how I was going to feed and clothe myself after being a convicted felon. The hardest time was returning to a church that was not ready or did not know how to restore a person that was once a member of the family of faith but was now considered a (lost) sinner. I was not lost, I was broken, I was injured, I was medically depressed not lost. The hardest times were experiencing fellowship with people that were trying to breakdown a vessel that had already been broken. A lot of the confidence and joy that I walked around with was because I was still young and no longer in a Floridian jail. That confidence though was merely an overshadow to the sensitive broken soul I really was. I was in need of a doctor and the counseling support from my Christian family was not there and if it was there I did not know how to recieve it. My happy go lucky demeanor was masking the real pain I lived in. Deep down I felt like a loser even though I had already paid my debt to society.

My experience going back to the church that I grew up in was like going to the hospital to see the doctor but, because I was not profusely bleeding near death, I was asked to have a seat in the waiting room. In some people's eyes if I did not wait in the waiting room for them to attend me, then I must have been full of pride. Surely I was full of pride at the young age of 24 but I was also broken. I hid my pain well. It really wasn't pride but a wall of self defense. I had lost so much trust over time that I felt that I could not open up to just anyone. I needed friendship from the church and I never got it or I was to hurt to be able to recieve it. One thing about the enemy of faith is that he does not have a waiting room. The enemy of the faith is always available and ready to steer God's children in his direction making them feel comfortable with drugs and alcohol. That would be the case I would suffer through for years. Self medicating the pain of not being restored properly to society or a church that manifested the truth. That hurt more than doing time. When I did attend church I had faith during the preaching but minutes after the preaching was over, I started to see things in a totally different picture. I felt I was no longer a part of the fellowship, I just did not ever feel comfortable, the enemy had me in shame. . I always felt as if I never did enough and God was never pleased with me.

Some folks in the church thought of themselves either to highly spiritually or too afraid to get close to me. It may or may not have been the intention of others to make me feel that way but that is the way I felt. We were definitely not on one accord as I had been when I was with the prisoners. One thing the prisoners and I had in common was that we all wanted to get out of jail as changed men for Jesus. We shared our peace during and after church service because we had to live with each other after service. The joy that I saw in some of the church folks now was not for Jesus's commission of sharing in His love and restoration for others but for the blessing of what they had attained for not getting punished for their sins as I had. Had the joy been for the victory that God gave us all at the cross or the message of hope towards others been more real after service then I would have been treated differently but I no longer felt that I fit in nor could I share my knowledge about what Christ had done in me. One personal complex that I had was that during my incarceration I had nearly lost it all. I had very little material possessions and money and I felt embarassed going to church. I was always a giving person even in my youth. So for me not to be able to give was embarassing to me. The enemy was having a field day reminding me of how even in some churches nowaday, the impression is about material success in order for people to deal with you. The devil is a liar though. Ministry/loyal brotherhood is not about the material possessions or titles. Ministry/loyal brotherhood is about maturing in the pure love of Christ to help our neighbors and the weak get strong in Christ. We should tend to everyones needs regardless of their appearance because we really do not know the debts of pain or hardship some people have been through or are going through. By the time I started thinking this way I had stopped attending church and was now carrying this burden on my shoulders.

Romans 14:17(KJV)

17 For the kingdom of God is not meat and drink; but righteousness, and peace, and joy in the Holy Ghost.

The healing process which God had started 1 year earlier, the enemy of my soul was now working hard to destroy. The enemy was about to try to steal every joy and hope that God had given me for a new life. Guilt and anger began to set in and although I was home now for about a year the enemy continued making me feel like a prisoner, like a convicted felon. It is one thing to be a convicted prisoner with the hopes of forgetting your past. It's another thing to absorb the guilt of being a convict. That guilt makes you feel like a reject from both society and the church. And these feeling I had were all brought on by the enemy through the traumatic experiences I had just gone through from my actual incarceration, my church experience and now the intoxication of my mind by medicating all my pain, my way.

In reality God's promises were coming to pass because He had blessed me with a good job six months after I relocated and for a year I worked counseling court mandated youth in a day program steered at helping troubled teens. It was a tough job dealing with so many youth that were so troubled. I gave them the hope that I had for a better life but deep down I was the one hurting. I felt spiritually incomplete by no longer fellowshipping with other mature Christians. Once the guilt and shame sets in you better hold on because you are about to go on a major detour and sadly that is what happened to me. As much as I knew I needed help, I did not know how to ask for it. The pressure of working with court mandated kids that were total delinquents weighted heavy on me. These kids were very strong to breakdown, they were very disrepectful to there own parents so imagine the outbursts of wrath and behaviors staff had to go through to get them to be kind. They had seen and done it all by the ages of 13-18. I was making good money but I was so drained mentally and spiritually that I ended up turned to alcohol and later to drugs to ease my pain, I could never ask for forgiveness enough for going back to a world that I knew God had already set me free from. I knew as a child of God that my temple was the dwelling place of the Holy Spirit but I was letting the enemy win and I did not know how to defeat guilt, shame and now addiction. It was a bad place to be.

The bible says, "be angry and sin not" do not let the sun go down on your wrath. Nor give place to the devil. Eph.4:26-27. But that is exactly the path that my guilt and shame was leading me on (sinning against myself). I was not committed to the faith that I needed the most to keep me strong. I did not know how to commit or submit. It was so hard for me to trust anyone. I had so many underlying issues of anger but my nice guy personality would always hide all those frustrations until I was out in the world by myself. Without Christ in my life the anger, depression and guilt was taking control of me making me sick in my mind and body. The pride of me being a survivor of incarceration did not allow me to go and get the help that I needed. I was a macho man, that was self destructing. It would only be a matter of time before the full manifestation of the my own destructive behavior would take over from time to time and put me in great dangers and in many distressing painfilled nights. I don't want to give the devil any glory by writing exactly the things I did but the things I did to myself were painful and wrong and if something is wrong to you, then bible says that it is sin.

Romans 14:22-23(KJV)

22 Hast thou faith? have it to thyself before God. Happy is he that condemneth not himself in that thing which he alloweth.

23 And he that doubteth is damned if he eat, because he eateth not of faith: for whatsoever is not of faith is sin.

I knew my sinful nature was getting more reckless and the more I sinned the weaker I got. I was now addicted to the pain of my depression and guilt. I tested God's patience, I am sure to His very limits in my self destructive behavior. I wanted to see how long it would take before God would strike me down. I did not really want God to strike me down but in a drunken state of mind I really did not care at all for anyone or even my faith in God, I was more than angry I was mad at life. After every episode I would go repent and God would forgive me each and every time but God's word says that He is not mocked and what a man sows that shall he reap. I continued to reap misery. If I had a food addiction and continually asked God to forgive me for overeating He surely will forgive me but the consequences of me continuing to overeat would be evident. My poison fruit was so much worse than just being overweight, my core fruit was depression and sometimes very suicidal thoughts and acts of trying to end it all with poisoning myself tormented me.

Galations 6:7

7 Be not deceived; God is not mocked: for whatsoever a man soweth, that shall he also reap.

Through it all somehow I had faith that in God's timing that he would fully heal my depression and take away all my pain someday. So many times God restored me enough to function on a day to day basis that I should have been more grateful but addiction and depression has its way of convincing the addict that it's ok now, it's safe to drink or hang out again with your friends and the cycle never ends that way. You need the power of the Holy Spirit to end it with an exclamation point at the end!

With me working full time my life started to become more normal and I was starting to settle into becoming a good hard working citizen. But the demons of my past were not done with me yet and it seemed that in order to get my life back I would soon have to go out on an all out spiritual war cry. When things continue going bad in your life and you know deep in your heart that all you want to do is good and live life for a better tomorrow you best believe that the attacks that are coming your way are demonic. The enemy of God just wants you to give up on your faith in Jesus Christ.

The enemy has limited power and the only way he can continue to destroy lives is if we let him. I believe the devil knows who the major threats to his kingdom of misery/darkness are but he does not know when these people will build their faith strong enough in Christ to be affective at destroying his works and proclaiming the day of salvation to others. So the enemy works his hardest to try and disrupt your peace and patients while you are a baby in Christ or are recovering from previous attack. He tries to work on your last nerve until you get tired of seeking God and instead blame the true and living God for all of your troubles.

Don't let him win! Remember you are in a spiritual fight against a spiritual enemy. Stand strong always in faith knowing that God is on your side.

Ephesians 6:10-13 (KJV)

Finally, my brethren, be strong in the Lord, and in the power of his might.

11 Put on the whole armour of God, that ye may be able to stand against the wiles of the devil.

12 For we wrestle not against flesh and blood, but against principalities, against powers, against the rulers of the darkness of this world, against spiritual wickedness in high places.

13 Wherefore take unto you the whole armour of God, that ye may be able to withstand in the evil day, and having done all, to stand.

CHAPTER 7

THE POWER OF PRAYER-UNIQUENESS

Through all the ups and downs in my own personal life I continued to work as a social worker helping handicapped adults have a more full life. But in my own life, I continued to struggle with severe depression mainly always ending in self medicating to ease away the pain when I could not handle it. Some of the few things I did positively to ease my pain was attend church, join a fitness gym and practice kneel down prayer from time to time at church and at home. Through all these positive community doors that were opened, kneel down prayer in my private time was where I really started to see God working in my life. Things were not always perfect but the good days always outweighed the bad days. My wife and I began attending church regularly on Sundays and soon we both began attending prayer night service on Tuesdays. I was feeling great and recognized that my joy and strength was still only found in the Lord. I was finally getting back the peace of mind and presence of the Lord that I had lost for so many years.

Ephesians 3:14-21King James Version (KJV)

14 For this cause I bow my knees unto the Father of our Lord Jesus Christ,

15 Of whom the whole family in heaven and earth is named,

16 That he would grant you, according to the riches of his glory, to be strengthened with might by his Spirit in the inner man;

17 That Christ may dwell in your hearts by faith; that ye, being rooted and grounded in love,

18 May be able to comprehend with all saints what is the breadth, and length, and depth, and height;

19 And to know the love of Christ, which passeth knowledge, that ye might be filled with all the fullness of God.

20 Now unto him that is able to do exceeding abundantly above all that we ask or think, according to the power that worketh in us,

21 Unto him be glory in the church by Christ Jesus throughout all ages, world without end. Amen.

As I felt many years of depression finally leaving, I started to believe in the power of prayer so much that I continued to pray on a daily basis every morning as I once used to when I was behind bars. The way the Lord began moving in my life was immediate. I was no longer faithless nor depressed, I was feeling hopeful. I was studing the word of God daily and I surely felt God's presence in my affairs. I rededicated my life to prayer, bible study and Godly living. I was working full and part time with people with special needs, I was thriving and I really did enjoy my day job helping others in need of care or counseling, whom could not take care of themselves. One very cold Tuesday night while attending prayer night service. I took off my scarf while getting ready for some kneel down prayer time as I had often done so in the past. I decided to fold my scarf in such a way that it would give me padding on my knee area and it would not take up too much space. That night my knees were happy that they did not have to endure the pain of hard cold wood flooring. As I began to pray immediately God said "you are blessed", I said "Amen thank you Jesus." Again I heard the Spirit of the Lord say, "you are blessed by folding your scarf so you can pray longer in comfort." I said "Amen thank you Jesus." I continued to pray while God was ministering to me internally telling me that he was happy that I was coming to church on Tuesday to fellowship with the brothers and sisters of the church. God was happy with me that I was choosing to pray and fellowship with my family of faith at the house of God rather than being out with my friends wasting time really doing nothing, as I had done so many times in the past.

As I continued to pray the Spirit of the Lord was heavy on me and I heard Him say, "I have seen your pain and suffering but I have also seen your giving and your faith and heart towards me and others." He continued "I am going to bless you out of these four walls if you decide to step out in faith." I said," Amen yes Lord." What do you require of me, He said," prayer and faith." I said," Lord you know that I have faith and I already continually pray what is required of me". He said "get my people to take prayer seriously" I said "ok and how shall I do that." He said, "the scarf you folded will help give comfort to people that are fearful of knee pain." He continued, "take the measurements of the scarf because I want you to design a prayer pillow that is stylish for this generation and will remind the young people to pray." I joyfully said "Amen!", I was now getting excited that God was giving me a revelation and I was hoping that this idea was part of what was going to get me out of my 9 to 5 and working instead full time in ministry. When I got this idea from God I ran with it. The next morning I drove around town looking for sew shops that could make a prayer pillow like God had given me the idea to design. The instructions from God were that it had to be lightweight, stylish, portable and able to open and close like a book with a handle attached to it. The uniqueness of the kneeler/prayer pillow was all those qualities but mostly that it opened and closed like a book, it was to be made in many colors and shapes, so children would want to use them, as well. That was the patent design that I got from heaven. And that is exactly what I set out to make. A unique, stylish, lightweight, portable and colorful prayer pillow.

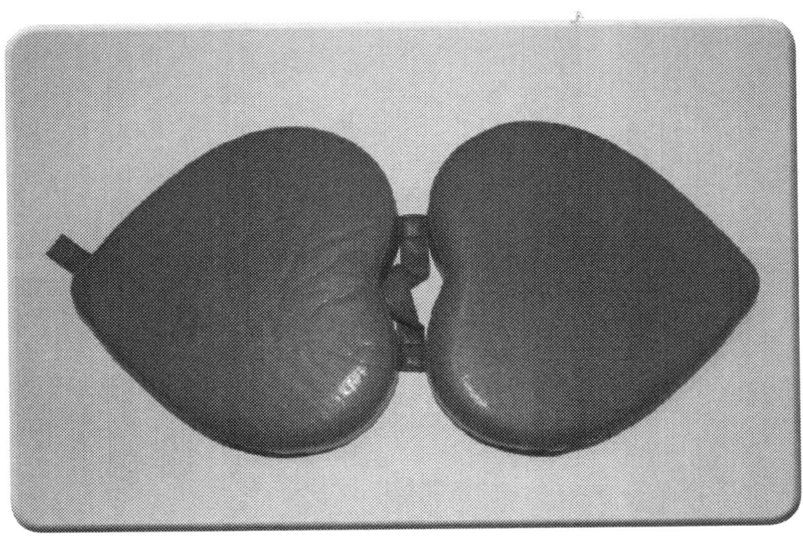

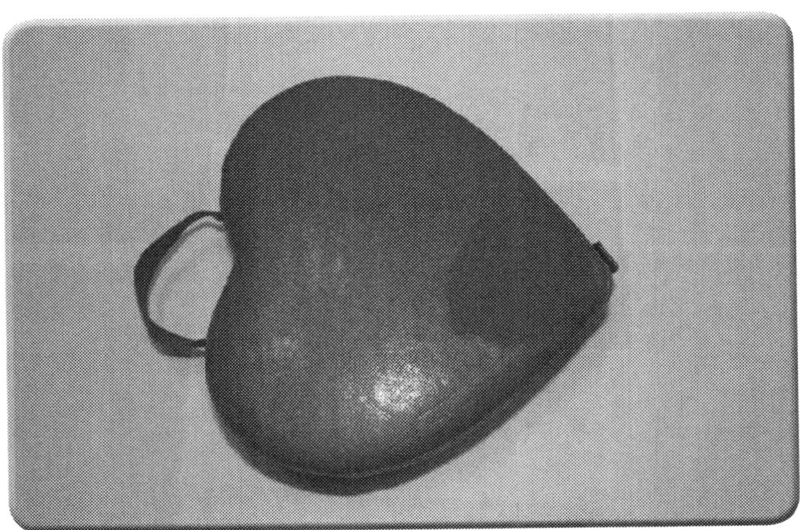

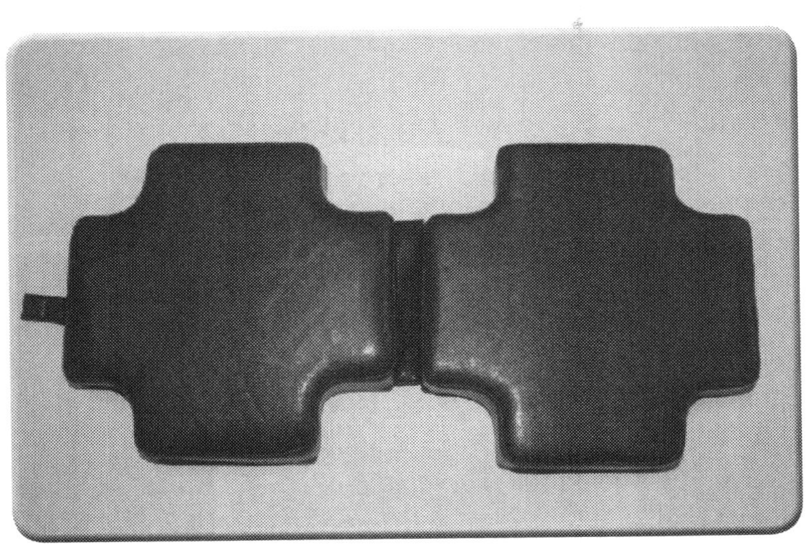

The first kneeler prayer pillow I made was designed at a boat repair shop in Norwalk, CT. It cost me $60 to have my design come to life. As I explained to the seamstress what I was doing with this design and who it was for excitement flooded my heart. I was so excited about creating something that I did not care what the cost was. I was now being creative for God and I was excited about the potential of what this unique prayer cushion pillow could be, not only for ministerial purposes, but how financially rewarding it could be for myself and my family. I always wanted to make my family proud, being that I had lost so many years of my life to depression and at times lived my life with no purpose. I was no college graduate but prayer and faith was about to qualify me for a position I would have never gotten on my own. CEO of my own company.

I continued to pray every day after work wondering how I was going to convince anyone to buy a prayer pillow from me if they were costing me $60 to make. Surely I had to make a profit as the designer/developer and by the time I got done perfecting, marketing and packaging the kneeler it would probably retail over $100 in value. I knew deep in my heart that I had to get the cost down somehow. God gave me this unique idea so I could earn a living while doing the work of a minister (sharing the good news gospel). In the bible there is a story about a king that gives out talents(money)Matthew 25:14-30. The king gave these talents to three people expecting them to make a profit. In the end two of the three people made a profit. The one that did not make a profit and was even fearful to put the money in the bank to earn interest was eventually punished. The ones that made a profit were rewarded with land. So the moral of the story is that when God gives you a talent or money you are to invest it wisely to make a profit. The profit should be used wisely to help others in need world wide.

As much as I did not want to look for manufactures overseas to make this unique prayer pillow I really had no choice. I could not afford to have these pillows made here in the USA. The only other forseeable problem was how was I going to have this unique prayer pillow made overseas if I don't know anyone overseas. I continued to pray, this time God said, "everything needed to make these unique pillows shall be found locally." I said "Amen ok thank you Jesus I trust in you." Not even a week goes by when I came to find out that my employment manager who was also my dear friend, was married to the man that has companies in China where they can develop and perfect my idea at less than half the cost. Isn't God good? My manager's husband was a huge blessing because I really had no idea on where to start. He held my hand during the whole process basically. He always reassured me that my idea could be perfected. He made a number of different colorful samples at no cost to me and that alone was a huge blessing to me. When I finally agreed on what styles I was going to go with, it would also be time to place that order. The only challenge now was that I needed to order the four different styles of kneelers at a quantity that was no less that a cargo container full. A cargo container is the big metal box that you see on cargo ships that transport everything from China to USA. That box comes in three sizes large, larger and largest. The largest cargo box was able to hold 12,000 kneelers. I had to get the smallest of the 3 if I was to make these kneelers affordable to the general public. The least I could order was 4000 kneelers at a time, one thousand of each of the four styles. It would take 3 months to manufacture in China and transport to the USA.

Now all I needed was to come up with forty thousand dollars which I did not have. I don't even think I had four hundred dollars in the bank let alone forty thousand. I had just paid a patent attorney five thousand dollars to protect my design, it was that unique. I did not even make 40 thousand dollars a year. How was I going to get these kneelers from China to USA? All I had was faith that this prayer pillow idea was from God and hope that he would make a way out of no way. I continued to pray and God continued to bless me daily telling me everything was going to be achievable. The passion for prayer never left me during the whole process in fact I knew and still know now that prayer and faith are the key to unlocking your greatest dreams and potential.

There was no way I was going to let this dream fade away due to money. I know that the God I serve is an awesome God and he would make a way out of no way. I had so much faith that the prayer pillow idea would be a great tool to encourage reverent prayer time for children and adults of all ages. I also knew that I had to get them made and manufactured overseas even if I had to come up with all the investment money myself. I reached out to a few churches for investors but I could not find any. People asked me for a business plan and all sorts of questions that I was not prepared for. I simply wanted to make a product that I believed was Holy Spirit inspired and hoped God would touch people to help me make it happen but that was not the case especially when you are seeking forty thousand dollars. You need a business plan in the world of business and to really educate yourself in business, not just faith in your ability, before making such an investment. In my ignorance I strickly ran on faith. I had no choice but to trust God that no matter how much debt I put myself in, that this was a great idea to invest in and God would provide and also bless my business. After praying and believing God, I had a sit down with my wife and sought her advice. She did not have the faith that I had but she was not totally against the idea. Her main concern was my health and well being. She liked the unique prayer pillows and was hopeful but the thought of taking out loans and maxing out credit cards to get the kneelers manufactured overseas sounded like a bit too much. She gave me a half hearted approval but it was still an approval. So the next day I went to the bank and took out a second mortgage for 25k . With that amount I was able to place the order. I now had 3 months to come up with the 15k balance. As the months passed I just continued to work my full time and part time job saving as much as I could. I was able to save one thousand but I was still 14k short. That was quite a bit of a shortage. I was really starting to worry about getting the other part of the money but I had alot of faith and just continued to believe God.

The money I had hoped for was not coming from anywhere and I now had only weeks to pay off the balance. To my advantage I had excellent credit at the time with my credit cards and I knew I could draw at least five thousand from my credit card accounts but I was still going to be short 9k with only a week to pay off my balance to the manufacturer. I would not give up on my faith, I had gone too far now and I had no choice but to ask my mother in- law if she could help. She was so gracious that she let me borrow the 7 thousand that I needed but it was still not enough. I was now days away from having to make the last payment and the final option I had to get all the money was to sell my car. As much as I loved my new car which was a beautiful gold colored 2002 Nissan Altima, it was also the first car I had ever bought at 0 miles. I now was willing to sacrifice and sell it in order to get the money I needed to go after my faith based ministry and business. I really trusted God to provide for me with transportation to and from my day job if I sold my car that week. Well my trust in the Lord and prayers worked because I sold my car a few hours after putting up a for sale sign. The car was not even parked anywhere visible yet God sent a buyer. The man who bought my car was visiting a neighbor and saw my car in the driveway. He saw the for sale sign I had just recently put on the vehicle with my number on it and called me. The gentleman told me that as soon as the bank opened in the morning he would buy my car. No test drive, no questions asked simply "I will buy your car". I told the gentleman that I was selling my car to invest my money in ministry that encouraged prayer through a uniquely styled prayer pillow that I designed. He thought it was a great idea and said "see you in the morning". I was in total shock but I was grateful to God who makes things possible even in the last minute of the day. The next day as the man promised he called me with the money, he had cash in hand and I sold my car for 6k that day. I now had enough money to pay off the balance of the kneelers and enough money to pay off the small balance that I owed on my car. God is good. In 3 months I came up with 40 thousand and the kneelers were on their way home from China.

I sacrificed my car for a dream of starting a good ministry and business for God. Only time would tell if the sacrifice was worth it but for now my father helped me out by giving me his 93 Nissan Pathfinder that had 190 thousand miles on it. The truck was old but not bad for getting around town. That truck moved well on the highway even though it had 190 thousand miles on it. It was not bad looking, but it was not my Nissan Altima. It did its job of getting me from point A to point B. I was ready to ride that truck until the wheels fell off.

CHAPTER 8

FINALLY HERE

Determined not to let anything stop me from encouraging prayer and faith in Christ, I had my mind set, but the enemy had other plans on derailing my confidence. Not long after making the biggest faith investment decision of my life, my faith would soon be tested by the breakdown of my gifted vehicle. The breakdown was so unlike any other problem I had ever had with a vehicle before. The motor was great, the transmission was perfect but the rear wheels where really about to fall off. I could not believe the unrepairable damage that it had due to an aging rust problem. The whole undercarriage of the truck was rotting away and the truck was unsafe to drive. At anytime both rear wheels could have fallen off if I attempted to drive it any farther. I only got to enjoy the 4x4 a few weeks before I had to junk it. It was hard to junk a vehicle that had an excellent motor and transmission but it had to be done because it was unsafe to drive. I did not have time to part out the truck so I just junked it. The damage was not visible unless you looked underneath the truck it was very dangerous to drive having all the rust damage from underneath. Once again I was left with no car but at least my wife had her car and we would share this car to get to work. Somehow it worked out until I was able to save up and buy a cheap car advertised online.

The time was moving quickly and before I knew it the kneelers had arrived and were finally here. The truck delivering my kneelers that pulled up to my house was the kind that you see on most highways hauling those really large containers. Now that small size container I ordered looked huge and barely fit in my driveway. Luckily I had my wife, nephew and mother to help me unload the boxes. We spent hours unloading the 335 boxes. I had kneeler boxes everywhere. My garage was at full capacity and now I needed to store some of these kneelers in my house. The boxes we unloaded took up two rooms in my home and the entire garage. Looking around I thought O boy! What did I get myself into? In spite of all the room the kneelers took up in my house I was still extremely happy that I got them right on time. As I opened the boxes to inspect the product, Wow! All I could say was what a great job my friend and friends did overseas for me. The kneelers were perfect. They were made just how I had envisioned them that cold February Tuesday night at church service when I first got the idea. That my friends is faith manifested!

Promotion Time

When it was time to start promoting the kneelers. I was in a time of my life of much excitement and hope for what the future was going to hold for me. I felt like my faith was lining up with everything the preacher was speaking concerning faith in Christ and also prospering as a Christian. I believed it back then and I believe it now that the kneelers that God gave me to encourage kneel down prayer is a good work and very marketable for this day and time. I blindly thought that everyone in church or in ministry was on the same page as me. I had no idea that the faith I had just put into manufacturing some unique prayer pillows for the glory of God was to be tested by the hands of leaders that did not understand my call to encourage reverent kneel down prayer with my unique pillow. Many did not support/ understand or chose not to understand my call to encourage kneel down prayer when using kneelers or fervent prayer to advance the Kingdom of God. I was soon to learn that not everyone around me believed in the power of prayer as I did nor the Kingdom of God through reverent prayer as I did.

Many around me smiled in my face and wished me blessings but failed to connect with the vision God gave me to encourage prayer. At times that made me feel abondoned and alone in my belief of God and the true honor we should give God almighty. I expected everyone to have the same passion and commitment to prayer as I did but I would soon find out that was not the case. We all have a call to advance God's Kingdom here on earth, but we are not all called to do the same thing. You will know your heavenly call when you have passion for that one thing that no one else does but you want to do it at all cost for the Lord. If you have already found your passion I pray that the Lord will continue to strengthen you to keep going forward. We are all called to work together regardless of each others call in order to advance the Kingdom of God here on earth. Encouraging and loving one another is one of the biggest messages that we as believers should make as a prority regardless if we go to church or not. Our testimony, our faith in Christ Jesus teachings is peace and love for each other, let the world see it.

Most of the promotion I did for the kneelers, was done online through my accounts on various social network sites.

My idea was very unique and my friends list soon grew to over 2500 friends quickly with many Christians admiring my portable and stylish kneelers but I was having a tough time actually converting those friends into kingdom time kneelers owners. I did make some contacts through out the US that I am very grateful for but marketing and distribution has been one of my hardest task. I really had no idea of how else to market my kneelers. I would soon find out years later that the prayer pillow design was God's design but His plan included way more than marketing prayer pillows. If this was going to be a true ministry at the core about salvation and building a solid relationship with God through prayer. The devil was not about to give up any ground. I would have to learn to fight the good fight of faith at a new level if I ever wanted to prosper. Was I ready, was the question?

Even though I lacked knowledge about spiritual warfare and business marketing, I thought I was ready. The overwhelming truth was, that I was in desperate need of a mentor that knew exactly what I was going to go through or about to go through. The spiritual attacks placed on my life by the enemy were not only meant to kill my business/ministry but mainly me. The financial attacks placed on my life where ment to bury me forever. It did not take long for the loan bills to start adding up and panick to set in. Thoughts of failure took over my mind because I could not sell enough kneelers to keep up with the bills. How could I? There was only a small number of people looking for a product like this. I struggled in my quest to find such great people of faith. Thank the good Lord that my wife and I both worked full time jobs to keep up with the bills. The kneeler although it was a great product was not a sought out product by the average Christian. Many still do not know to this day that these stylish kneelers are available nor do they really know the importance of reverent prayer to fulfill their mission as a student of the gospel of faith. There is a major need for my product and the ministry of prayer. Many Christians do not get the support or do not know how to market their talent or gifts to other believers. I always believed Kingdom people took prayer seriously and supported each other in all things but we have let the world influence how we treat each other in business affairs. If you begin a project in a worldly mindset (the get rich quick mindset) you better be prepared as to what you are getting into being a Spirit filled believer. The world with all its fast paced marketing of any products makes things look easy, but it is not easy, especially being a believer, that is why we are to educate and take care of each other. You are either in the mainsteam to be known or you better work hard, work smart to let people know you are here. It cost alot of money and it takes alot of time to market anything new in this day and age. Be prepared, be warned for those who are beginner entrepreneurs. With that said, God wants you to prosper so fear not!

About the fourth or fifth month is when I really started to get emotionally off track. I was frustrated that the kneelers where not selling or getting picked up by any major distributors as I expected so they could be visible to the public. As I presented the kneelers to pastors, it seemed like pulling teeth to get some faith based support. At Christian events most people would walk right past my booth as if I was not there. The ones that did stop by and chatted with me loved the idea and design, I did sell a few that way but it was very time consuming almost not even worth the sacrifice to get the overpriced vendors booth at any event. The reviews were always great towards the product but it was very hard to market with out having a platform or more importantly having the people of God wanting to pray more on their knees. The kneelers which I praised God so much about, thanking him for giving me such a great idea was now about to put me through some very difficult test. My personnal faith in God was about to be tested on every level by fire once again. God never called me to be the door to door salesman of prayer pillows, I was supposed to just put this product out on the market and let every man, woman, or child decide if this product could help them, but without support from Christian retailers to give you that space to show case, it is impossible.

1 Corinthians 3:11-15(KJV)

For other foundation can no man lay than that is laid, which is Jesus Christ.

12 Now if any man build upon this foundation gold, silver, precious stones, wood, hay, stubble;

13 Every man's work shall be made manifest: for the day shall declare it, because it shall be revealed by fire; and the fire shall try every man's work of what sort it is.

14 If any man's work abide which he hath built thereupon, he shall receive a reward.

15 If any man's work shall be burned, he shall suffer loss: but he himself shall be saved; yet so as by fire.

CHAPTER 9

TROUBLE IS IN MY WAY. MOVE

The first relationship to encounter trouble was my marriage. I felt like a failure to my spouse and business partner. As much as I tried not to show my frustration and disappointment in regards to the impact as I had expected with the kneelers, my prayer life was starting to take second place. Little arguments about how I should have handled things became more frequent in my home. I was frustrated because it seemed like others were prospering doing nothing for God while here I was in a sinking ship with no one around to help me. There was no one holding my hand able to assure me that everything was going to be ok. The frustration was manifesting due to the loans that were taken out in both mine and my wife's name. The loans were all due and now my giving to the church was going to suffer cut backs so I could survive to pay my bills. It was a trial of my faith. Most of my life I have been a giver even when I was a faithless sinner. I loved to share when I had money and do my part to help support the needy.

But now I was going to be the one living on just enough because the kneelers were not selling. That bothered me greatly.

I wondered where was the support of the mega-churches and all the ministries that I sowed thousands of dollars into for years all across the USA listening to their sermons on prosperity were? I reached out, sent samples, sent letters to churches, made phone calls but nothing in return. The same went with some smaller local churches. Everything that happens all across the world whether good or bad begins at the church.

17 For the time is come that judgment must begin at the house of God: and if it first begin at us, what shall the end be of them that obey not the gospel of God? 1 Peter 4:17 KJV

I feel grieved having to share my disappointments with the church were I know prayer is number one. I never expected any one ministry to bail me out, just a little support would of went a long way. Any one of them could of gifted these prayer pillows to their congregation and God's blessing would of multiplied. The reality is people are hurting and frustrated after giving so much and expecting God is going to bless the giver within the congregation. As a member of both a local church and an online member/supporter that gives, I have a voice. If we are all part of one body in this faith walk then we have to support one another, who else is called to support one another but the church itself. Is the body of Christ more than just an arm or a leg, I tell you not.

> 21 And the eye cannot say unto the hand, I have no need of thee: nor again the head to the feet, I have no need of you.
>
> 22 Nay, much more those members of the body, which seem to be more feeble, are necessary:
>
> 23 And those members of the body, which we think to be less honourable, upon these we bestow more

abundant honour; and our uncomely parts have more abundant comeliness.

24 For our comely parts have no need: but God hath tempered the body together, having given more abundant honour to that part which lacked.

25 That there should be no schism in the body; but that the members should have the same care one for another.

26 And whether one member suffer, all the members suffer with it; or one member be honoured, all the members rejoice with it.

27 Now ye are the body of Christ, and members in particular. 1 Corinthians 12:21-27 KJV

An Emember is just as much a member of the church and the body of Christ as any other believer and treatment should be no less.

So I preferred to stay home suffering silently rather than go to church and feel like a failure. I was starting to cave in slowly and I knew that I was going to be in for a long ride. My prayer to God was, forgive me for not fellowshipping with my brothers, but I do not want to be bitter and start blaming them or those ministries I supported, because I knew it was not there fault that I did not get my breakthough as I expected, but who was I to really blame? God, Myself, or the church. I was now officially in the race of doing something big for God and the bigger the project the more I needed to pray. I chose self pity and anger. That was a big mistake for me. I can now say that because now I am in a better place, but back then the test of fire was inevitable. When trouble like this comes your way, don't worry, God understands that you are only human and have your limitations. Just try not to give the enemy any ground by being angry with your brothers, God, or yourself. Just continue to pray until the storm ends. Pray everyday, pray every chance you get and just be grateful to the Lord for all things, until you get your strength back. The test is only a trial of your faith to see if you are going to be courageous enough to fight the way God teaches us to fight in His word. If you come back to your call, then just consider it a delay not a denial. You are still going to have to continue pushing yourself, to make your dream a reality. If you decide to move on with something else that is also fine but just keep going forward with God. You are not a failure. Maybe, God has something better for you up ahead. Keep going forward to get the best out of life because the God of peace is still there, regardless of how we feel.

When I finally let go of my call, I let go of my church too. I was still a Christian I just did not behave like one. I started to behave like an angry child that did not get his way. Was I justified to behave like this? Maybe. But God certainly did not want me to justify my actions. God wanted me to trust in Him. The bible says that "the just shall live by faith" especially if things are not going your way. The just shall live by faith until your breakthroughs manifest. Got it. Good! I sure wish I would have had that mind set back then. Not having that mind set to continue to have faith and pray lead me to years of leaving my call. (years)

When your health and finances are in bankruptcy you begin to realize how real this spiritual battle is. Before my finances went bankrupt, I was spiritually bankrupt. I gave up and I was now trying to fit in again into the world. Broke, busted, and disgusted. At times, the misery had me just were it wanted me. Depressed, angry, smoking, drinking, and gambling once again with the world as if I never knew God. I still continued to pray, but now it was because I was a sinner in need of his mercy time and time again. I prayed at times I did not lose my job after staying out late and calling in sick the next day, it was pure misery and depression giving up on God. It seemed like I had no choice though. That is not the call of us saints to live. God has called us to walk in victory overcoming sin and temptation daily regardless of what is going on around us or even in us. We can walk in victory we just have to stay focused no matter what comes our way. God asks us to be wise in all things not just when things are going good. We have to take care of our temples to keep our mind focused on overcoming every hurdle that comes our way.

Years started to go by and my kneelers continued in storage. It bothered me greatly and even though I was not going to church nor praying, I still knew in my heart that God had some prayer warriors in houses that could benefit from using my prayer pillows. I disliked having my kneelers locked away in storage. I had thousands of them neatly stored. I wish I did not have to see them in there. I preferred giving them away. So I started to give away a bunch of kneelers to churches in hopes that I would maybe hear back from some of them, yet nothing ever happened. I was numb to the disappointment. I knew I had a great product but not even a thank you or a follow up phone call. Ever! People love stuff for free especially church folk. They never really know the price some people have to pay in order for them to get their free stuff. Some things cost someone their bankruptcy, their divorce or even their life! It's sad to think that as Christians in this day and age we don't use the spirit of discerment to notice when (1 Corinthians 2:14) someone needs help. We simply forget to ask. Do you need help? Is there anything I can do for you? It's even sadder when it's ministers in leadership positions that forget to ask these questions?

Three years had now passed and things were just stagnant. I lived with a very heavy heart from time to time. Always questioning the what if. At times I would take out my kneeler and pray and everytime I finished praying I would always thank God for my kneeler and tell myself I don't care what anyone says the kneelers are a very great idea for this day and age. How could this fail? That was alway the question that baffaling my mind. I often thought God you called me to this. How could your abandon me now? God always wanted me to stay in ministry, I just did not want it anymore. I was hurt long enough and I was just hoping to move on. I did not know what I was to move on to but I just wanted to move on.

Five years after filing for bankruptcy, nearing my thirteenth year of employment as a direct care worker, and a couple of days before Christmas. I had an incident with one of my clients that would cost me my job. I knew the enemy was still out to destroy me. There was no doubt about that. This attack came out of nowhere and here once again, it was life repeating itself. I had an excellent job and I was loved and respected by many, but one bad day at the office sent me to the unemployment line. Everything that I worked so hard for in my secular career was now down the drain too. I was terminated on January 6, 2011. Six days into the new year. Happy New Year seemed so ironic. I lost three weeks of paid vacation, my health insurance, my dignity, and all faith in the integrity of employers. I was now completely overwhelmed and almost overtaken by the enemy to the point of suicide.

In the bible there is a story about a man named Job that lost it all, never committing any sins. He was so righteous in God's sight that God allowed the devil to turn his life into pure misery. Only to prove to the devil, that Job really loved God no matter what. In the end of the story Job recovered all the devil had stolen or destoyed by double portion blessings from God. I certainly was no sinless Job but I used this story to not lose my mind or faith in God, during this horrible time in my life. It is a great story that I strongly recommend people read if they are going through some heartbreaking losses, the book of Job is found in the old testament bible.

Through my greatest trial of failing at my business and ministry, leaving the church, and losing my job. I always remembered the book of Job and tried very hard to keep the very little bit of peace that I had with God and like Job never cursing God or blaming him. If anything I always knew I had a relentless adversary that one day God would make him pay me back every cent he had stolen from me. With very little strength on hand I still believed God had a purpose despite all the losses and suffering. I just didn't feel like praying anymore after I lost my job. Yet this was the time when I should have been praying the hardest. I just convince myself that I didn't care anymore. I was numb to pain. I cried so much when I failed with the kneelers that I just didn't care if I lived or died. Amazingly somewhere deep inside of me I had a peace that I did not understand or ask for, but was there. I was not crying out to God, why me Lord, why me. I always felt that I did my job effectively in ministry, business, and secular work and I was not going to let the devil kill me with depression once again. In this great trial all I saw was disappointment and I was not the author of it. I refused to engage with sadness, instead I choose to wait. Very aware of the news on how bad the economy was getting and all the jobs that were being lost in 2011. I did not feel alone.

Luckly my wife was working full time and I still had a part time job that gave me just enough income to cover all our bills. I certainly did see God's hand in our affairs in even in our darkest hour. My wife and I still loved each other and that was part of my survival and strength, even when I had none.

No business, no ministry, no church, no job, no health insurance and with everything down the drain, as if that was not enough, now my health was breaking down with severe stomach pains that just came out of nowhere. Could things get any worse? Weeks later I would find out the reason for the stomach pain. A blood clot! Of all places, the clot was located in my inferior vena cava. An important vein that carries blood from the body into the heart and lies right in the abdominal area. I needed treatment and a miracle from God to survive.

Mainly all of 2011, I threw myself one big giant pity party. I felt I had every right to. One can only take but so much. My motivation was at an all time low. I worked part time. Seeking fulltime work although halfheartedly because I had no desire to work helping mental health patients anymore. All my energy was drained physically and mentally and at the end of the day I had nothing to show for it but a pink slip. In my depression I gained 30 unhealthy pounds. My health was deteriorating suffering almost daily with stomach pains and the hospital bills were now quickly adding up.

Before my termination in 2011, I was in the gym working out playing basketball and lifting weights. I was really angry I allowed my termination to now also get me out of shape. By the end of 2011, I decided it was enough! I had a New Year's resolution for the up coming year with high hopes of at least starting to go back to the gym to work out and expected to get myself back in shape. I also had hope that I would get motivated enough to go seek after a good full time job in the process. Well the job never manifested after sending out my resume multiple times, but I did start working out hard. Within a month I had lost 10 pounds. I was starting to feel great, although I was taking prescribed blood thinners to treat my blood clot infirmity. I was starting to convince myself that maybe God had something special for me concerning fitness. I was certainly starting to feel all the benefits of exercising. Everyday depression was less and less. I had more energy, motivation, and confidence that things were going to get better. Into the second month of my indoor running someone on social media shared a link for a half a marathon that was three months away. So I began to pray about it and presented it to the Lord. Asking God to give me the strength to compete. I knew training for a half marathon would challenge me and keep me motivated. So I ran everyday pushing my body to the very limit one minute at a time, one mile at a time, sometimes with tears in my eyes because pushing your body to the limit hurts. I was determined to compete, and to finish the 13.1 miles. So I signed up to run my first half marathon at the age of 38.

On the day of my race I was 30 pound lighter after four months of training even though I was still a bit heavy for a runner at 230 pounds, which was now more musle. I finished the 13.1 miles and did good on timing for my first half marathon. I ran the half marathon in 2 hours and 21 minutes. God is good! I never though I could become a marathoner, but here I was stretching myself in faith to be a competitor and I did it, God gave me the victory. I was very proud of myself and the strength that God gave me to compete. Finally I was moving on from the kneelers, the loss of my job, and the depression that came from feeling like a failure. In the years to follow I continued training and running. I was able to compete in two more half marathons, as well as run 10k's (6.2miles) and many

5k's(3.1miles) to raise funds for local food pantries, people with disabilities and many charitable organizations. Each time my timing would improve. Here in New England us Latins are not really known for running, especially long distance running like marathons. Which made me very proud to be able to represent the small growing community of Latin runners. This was a great victory as a Christian and as a minority. Running makes me feel strong and free. There is drive and passion back in my life when I run or go for long walks. In a way running transports me closer to God's side. I look forward to running. Many times while training I would envision myself on this peaceful, beautiful, long road, green grass on both sides, the bluest of skies and the brightest sunshine. In the distance I am running towards an amazing palace like structure. In my vision I live there. When this vision comes to mind I always run faster and faster like I was running towards the kingdom. I truly believe God can change any of us as we dedicate our lives and temples to him. He sets the goals in our lives so we can experience Him at different levels and settings. When everything comes together mind, body, and soul we are complete in God. We can be more effective as true living testimonial lights for a world that needs hope and encouragement.

In September of 2012 I finally landed a full time job as a carsales man. It was a beautiful dealership but the hours were very demanding. I still had my part time job and was now working 7 days a week nearly 60 to 70 hours between both jobs. It seemed like all my marathon training was going to be put to good use working those type of hours. The problem was that I was not making the money that I felt I deserved and at times I started to losing interest. I was putting in so many hours at the dealership that I did not have time to go to the gym. That bothered me greatly. As I soon learned, a salesman's trade was making phone calls and reaching out to people I started to think maybe this is the approach I should have taken using the phones for my kneelers promotion. I knew it was not like selling a car, and maybe it was me who lacked that sales drive I needed to make the connections I needed. I never wanted to give too much thought to the what if's because I did not want to get depressed again but that thought never left me.

During my sales training I was shocked at how good I was becoming with making phone calls and pitching customers to come in to test drive the cars we had. Otherthan selling candies in school I had never really done sales before and it was exciting to me to speak with strangers everyday. Was God preparing me for something by teaching me how to be a confident and relaxed sales man? It sure seemed like it. Especially when I started to read a book called The Greatest Salesman by Og Mandingo. The book is about sales and it is faith based, which I found to be a very good read.

Into my fourth month as a car salesman, I seemed to be doing ok. I was still unhapppy with all the hours I had to work. And although I had nearly 30 cars sold by the end of my third month, I was losing interest. Old man Winter was on the horizon and the cold weather was starting to set in.

Cold weather and car sales is not a good mix. It did not take long for me to figure out that I was possibly headed into a very challenging season for sales. Was I up to the challenge or was I going to cave in? In all honesty the more I committed myself to working these long hours the colder the sales floor seemed. I said to myself, there has got to be a better way.

Matthew 11:28-30 (KJV)

28 Come unto me, all ye that labour and are heavy laden, and I will give you rest.

29 Take my yoke upon you, and learn of me; for I am meek and lowly in heart: and ye shall find rest unto your souls.

30 For my yoke is easy, and my burden is light.

CHAPTER 10

12-14-12

Friday December 14, 2012 started off as a usual day at the sales desk. The weather was a bit chilly and partly sunny. I remember getting two phone calls early that morning about two pending car deals I had been working on for weeks. Both customers called me around the same time and thanked me for being so kind to them as their salesman, but they no longer were interested in buying their new car at our dealership. I did not get much of an explaination as to why they were backing out. Maybe they both found a better deal or were interested in another type of vehicle that I could not offer. I was rather disappointed that I had just lost two deals back to back one hour into my work day. Eleven days before Christmas and now the money I was counting on for Christmas gifts had just gone out the window. When it was my turn to go on the sales floor, I was determined to get a sale that day. I desperately needed the money if I was at least to get my wife a decent Christmas gift.

Around 10:30am a young and very interested couple walked into the dealership. They seemed like the perfect couple and were ready to buy a car that day, I felt it. I remember going on the test drive with them, filled with excitement, confident that I had the sale I needed in my pocket. My feelings of excitement were correct. The couple I was pitching the new car to were ready to buy that day. They had perfect credit and no issues when it came to their income. As we all sat at my sales desk to prepare a contract, my laptop computer was signed into the MSN page. The first thing I noticed was there had been a shooting in Newtown,CT at an elementary school. I did not read all the details as it was still a developing story, but the little I read, did not seem good at all. My excitement of selling a car to the couple sitting in front of me immediately changed. The couple in front of me seemed to have noticed the change in my demeanor and asked me if everything was ok. I shared with them the news that there was a shooting at a school in Newtown and it seemed that many children were shot and killed. We were all in a sudden shock and saddened, but we tried to stay focused on finishing the deal. As I got up from my desk to go get a value appraisal from my manager for the couples trade in vehicle, a vivid image displayed on the news concerning the shooting, was embedded on my mind. It was a woman with her hand over her mouth, crying surrounded by emergency vehicles.

When I returned to my desk with the appraisal report, the numbers were not good at all. I knew I was on the verge of losing yet another sale that day. The deal that seemed so secure was no longer in my hands. The system the dealership used to appraise the trade in value gave the customer's vehicle an outrageous low number and although the number was low our job was to work out a deal. That was not going to be an option for the consumers as they already had a number they expected for their trade in. There was nothing I could do to secure the deal. The atmosphere was cold. The deal was going down the drain fast and I knew it. It was the third deal for me to go down the drain before noon. As the couple left the dealership without contract without a new car, all I could think about was that developing story out of Newtown. With my laptop still on I quickly went back to the page with the developing news. I began reading about the horrific tragedy that was going on just 40 to 50 minutes from where I was located. When I was done reading the MSN new report, regarding all that was happening that day in Newtown, I was saddened and sick to my stomach. I went to the rest room where I could be all alone to ask God why why? As I tried to pray and try to shed a tear for the community, I could not. My mind was consumed with just trying to sell cars. "You are a salesman! Now go out there and sell cars! That was the thought that continually rang out in my head as I tried to mourn. "You had your chance to do good. Why do you care about what is happening in Newtown?" Was all I heard. All I kept questioning myself about was, "Where is your prayer life now?" Confusion and anger followed as I could not understand what was happening. I was so upset at the fact that I could not focus. All I could think about was," not now devil", but it continued. At that moment I was, bitterly confused. I was angry at what was happening in Newtown and even angrier that the devil was basically laughing in my face as I tried to mourn for the lost children. I was very sad and concerned but everytime I tried to shed a tear I just couldn't. My heart was cold, why did it grow cold on this particular day? I do not know, I thought I was fine but in this moment all I had was cold memories of what it felt like to mourn with a community. What was wrong with me? When September 11, 2001 occured I don't think anyone in the world didn't shed a one tear including me, yet this new tragedy was equally horrific and devastating and here I was unable to produce tears to join our community in mourning.

I could not weep or cry out to God as I wanted to for those families that lost loved ones. I knew in my heart I was in the wrong place. Right at that moment I knew I was living a lie for these months, even years. I desperately realized I did not want to be that person any longer. I knew at that moment that for all these months and years I was living a lie and I desperately did not want to be the person anymore. I did not know who I was. I couldn't accept the fact that I was unable to mourn what I had just seen on the news. There was a time in my life when I was very sensitive to all that was happening all around me and I felt God close to my heart. But this time I was hearing laughter in my head and all I could think was, "Am I nuts to hear this laughter in my head?" "Was that me laughing or was that an evil spirit in or around me?" In my prior relationship with the deeper things of the Lord, I would have known it was the devil, but now I was in denial. To my amazement I could hear a voice of "who cares" about Newtown, clearer than hearing God's voice and love for a community that had just lost 26 lives.

That was it! I was done with this dealership job! I just wanted to run out of that dealership as soon as I could and never return! So that is exactly what I did. At 2 pm I left the dealership and quit my job on the spot without reason. I just walked out and told myself I was never coming back. The staff was always good to me but I had to go. I had some real serious underlying issues which I knew at that moment I had to take care of. It was almost as if I had a panic attack and I did not know what to do other than leave the building. So the next thing I did to drown out the noise in my head was make a stop at the wine and liquor store . While driving I continually asked God "why did this happen and why I couldn't I mourn over this tragedy?" Silence followed, for a bit then I heard "they were not my children why should I care?" That was what I heard and it made me feel horrible. Because I really did feel like I had lost a child, but here I couldn't even weep. I was sad, angry, and confused. I just wanted that incident out of my head but I could not shake it off. A dark cloud was over the entire nation that day and the confusion in my mind and those dark voices made me helplessly confused. Since I had no active prayer life, I began to drink while cursing the devil, the anger turned to severe depression over this tragedy. Alone in my car parked I continued to drown myself with alcohol. I could not even begin to imagine what the parents and loved ones of the victims were going through or going to endure through. I just kept thinking about my two young nephews that were both five years old at the time of the tragedy. That could have been them. What if it were them? What type of person could have killed 26 innocent people twenty of them being children. All I wanted to do was find a place to mourn on this horrific yet that place was nowhere to be found.

★a moment of silence for the Newtown CT shooting victims★

Crying out to God was the only way I would be able to mourn for the victims, the families, and community of Newtown, yet I was so upset I didn't know how to start. So as I continued on my drinking binge that night, I no longer cared about anything or anyone. Completely depressed and angry, I began shouting at God once again, "Why was I living to see this horrific day?" I was so mad at the devil for destroying another community especially a community of children. All I wanted was an answer from God, as to why this was affecting me so much, and what did my prayer life and kneelers have to do with this? The kneelers had nothing to do with the tragedy, so why was I constantly thinking about prayer? This thought tormented me, had I continued to pray and encourage prayer, maybe this tragedy would've never happened. That thought was so deep for me. The connection I once had with God through prayer felt so real, that at times. I felt like my prayers were making a difference in the community until I stopped.

That night, I did not care about Christmas being a few days away, unemployment, or anything else for that matter. I was in despair. Grieving without tears for the broken families and the young angels that departed to heaven too soon. I knew the families and our community were going through much pain. A life changing pain. A pain that doesn't fade or go away. I lived with that pain for many years until I encountered God for real long ago. He had taken all my pain away. But due to lack of maintaining connected to God, it hardned my heart so much that I no longer cared about anyone. But at this very moment in time I began to feel that pain all over again. I felt like I failed God for letting go of my faith and prayer ministry. And for refusing to fight for what I believed in. In this dark moment all alone in my car, I felt a weight and heaviness and a need to mourn with these families whom I did not know. I was so ashamed of who I had become by masking the pain with drugs and alcohol. I was ashamed of the Gospel that once had me so motivated for God. I was embarrassed of starting a prayer ministy for God and how it had failed horribly. What if I would have remained focused on my ministry? Would the shooting have ever occured? What could I have prevented if I took prayer seriously regardless of who believed in me or didn't? Who am I to even think these thoughts at a time like this. What misery and grief. Who am I Lord, and what are you trying to communicate to me. Please help me understand God! Please!

I had to find out what this all ment. I had to return to God with full faith as I had done so long ago. I wanted to return to God. The community that just lost loved ones would need true believers in God to help them get through this tragedy. I knew I was not ready to help in anyway but this was my time to change. Was it too late God? I didn't care. I had already quit my job. I was ready for a change Lord, please help me! My life was about to have it's biggest overhaul. I didn't care what it took I was not going to let the devil laugh at me anymore or get the last laugh! It is a terrible thing when God calls you and you are not ready to give an account. "God forgive me and give me strength, was my inner cry. I am ready to give my life back to you Jesus." Having no peace in my heart or in my mind, were the reasons I wanted and needed to change. "God! Please Help! Hear my humble cry."

The following days I began to pray fervently for the families of Newtown. I kept them in prayer for days and weeks to come. When the tears finally came out I could not stop. I wept for weeks for the families of the Newtown victims. Everyday with the remembrance of a smiling child gone to heaven too soon. What if that was my child that got killed?

In the new year of 2013 I entered in sober and prayerful. For the month of January all I did was fast and pray to God. Everyday I got on my kneeler and just prayed and wept for this nation. Always lifting up the families of the Newtown tragedy in prayer. Prayer became the number one priority in my life once again. The only time I left my house were to work my part time job, go for my daily run or walk all the while still praying and as soon as I was done with work, I was back to my prayer room. I called no one. I looked for no one. I really took prayer to heart as I had in 2007 and in 1996 when I was incarcerated. This time I had more passion because I knew in my heart what I had lost. I had a reason to pray not only for me but because of the evil that had visited Newtown, CT a month earlier.

After about a month of prayer, fasting, and watching preaching and teaching videos on youtube the passion and fire for God came back in my life. I did not attend any church for six months. All I did was seek God and have service on my own and in my own house. I stopped watching TV and listening to the radio. I did not care about the Hollywood stars or who was winning their next Grammy. That was of little importance to me, I just wanted to get my strength back because I knew I was going to have a devil to fight as soon as I integrated back into the community. Daily I would gain great strength all the while maintaining humble and reverent. Really dedicating myself to finding out who I was in Christ Jesus. During my many days and nights of prayer, I would often have nightmares as I tried to go to sleep during the first 3 weeks of praying. I would often have to get up in the middle of the night and go to my prayer room again and again to pray until I felt safe to go back to bed. I battled in that room for weeks with the evils of this world. I say the evils of this world because I was not living in sin any longer. Whether they were inner or outer demons I do not know, what I do know is that I was no longer sinning nor living in sin, but the battles I was facing were so intense, scary and sometimes very painful in my body, that I knew I was fighting evil spirits that roamed the earth and had caused my ministry to fail and my day job to be terminated. These spirit demons the bible calls anti-christ and false prophets are already here and keeping many believers from the real blessing and truth of knowing who we are in Christ. We believers are more than conquerors through Christ Jesus's love.

4 Beloved, believe not every spirit, but try the spirits whether they are of God: because many false prophets are gone out into the world.

2 Hereby know ye the Spirit of God: Every spirit that confesseth that Jesus Christ is come in the flesh is of God:

3 And every spirit that confesseth not that Jesus Christ is come in the flesh is not of God: and this is that spirit of antichrist, whereof ye have heard that it should come; and even now already is it in the world. 1 John 4:1-3 King James Version

After weeks of what seemed to be daily nightmares and spiritual attacks that would numb my body to the point where I could not even move or open my mouth. I felt helpless. I felt like a gagged and mute quadriplegic in my bed as I tried to sleep for breif moments. It was very frightening. Until one Saturday morning the Lord began to speak to me audibly. It was the greatest experience of my life and also the most frightening. The Lord's voice came to me one morning after having a horrible nightmare in which I was dying. The dream that lead me to hear God clearly was a bit strange but all so real. I dreamt that I was a passenger in a convertible car driven by my father. My father was driving me around in a late model vehicle around a mountain side curb that resembled The Grand Canyons in Arizona with it's high cliffs and deep valleys. It was a beautiful view but at the rate of speed that my father was driving we were sure to fly off the cliff. As my father continued to pick up speed driving around the curves, my heart began to race as the road seemed to get more narrow and narrow. So I yelled at him "slow down and watch out for the curves!", as I yelled, "watch out!", the car raced off the cliff and we went airborne as the car began descending, immediately my heart began racing so fast that I passed out at that moment. It felt now like I was in a dream within a dream expecting death if not already dead as we were falling at a high rate of speed. As I blacked out in the dream. I entered the black hole in space, it was super dark at first but as I traveled through the darkness. The darkness turned into hyperspace like atmosphere with tiny bright lights that resembled the stars in our outer space. I was no longer in my body, I was floating weightlessly. It was a very pleasant place. In my dream I heard a voice calling me by my name. The voice was powerful, loud, yet soothing. As I listened I kept hearing "Son, Son! You, are ok I am with you." Immediately I smiled as I thought I had died and was now alive with God. "Can you hear me?" I said yes Lord. Not audibly at first but in my thoughts I continued to say Yes. The voice replied: "good." The voice sounded as clear as if I had earphones plugged into my ears at high volume. I had such peace throughout my body and hearing that pleasant voice really awed me. I felt like I was floating in space while completely awake in my mind. It was the greatest experience in my life and I wanted to know was this God? I did not dare to ask, I just believed that it was. All I remember hearing was this crystal clear pleasant voice telling me that if I could hear His voice to repeat audiably the words, check one- two, check one- two. So I said out loud "check one- two, check one- two" this was all happening while I was physically sound asleep, but awake. Then I heard a voice again saying: "he can hear Us." This may sound funny and out of this world but this was a reality on that day! I felt like an astronaut in space talking to NASA while looking around in outer space trying to find something. At that moment if I opened my eyes I'd wake up, but I wanted to look around some more to see where I was and who was talking to me so I kept my eyes closed. Through faith, I knew it was the Lord because His presence alone was immensely peaceful, so I decided to open my eyes and get up out of bed. I was still not fully awake and it seemed I had not fully landed from this out of space experience because I was in total heavenly peace. I had the biggest smile on my face that I have ever had in my life. I could still hear the voice clearly telling me: God is with me. The joy of the Lord was so overwhelming. The peace and warmth I felt was incredible. I could not believe what I had heard and experienced in my life that day. I must have seemed nutty to my wife that morning as I sat at the kitchen table preparing my breakfast. With a giant smile on my face still in total awe, I kept hearing the voice clearly meanwhile I had a worship song in my heart that was continually blessing the Lord. It was as if my soul was internally singing with the angels and I was no longer in control but felt a great internal peace about it. By this time I knew the voice was of God or at least the Holy Spirit which is sent from God to comfort us. The voice said, " God has heard your prayers. We are always with you so fear not." Do you hear Me?" the voice questioned me again, this time as I sat dumbfounded in my kitchen. "If you hear me say check one- two audibly." I was sitting at my kitchen table with my mouth wide open in total shock. I was smiling from cheek to cheek, I proceeded to reply to the inner voice with check one- two. The voice said: "good he hears Us." The next thing I heard was just my mission statement from the Lord. The Lord reassured me that all of my sins were forgiven from the past and that they always were, don't ever walk around with guilt, you are forgiven through Christ Jesus. I heard the Lord telling me that I was working for Him and that I needed to continue to pray and seek God as often as I could. The voice told me that I was going to go through some very difficult tests in the future but not to fear, that he would not forsake me ever. "Keep going forward in faith," was all I kept hearing. "You are not always going to hear me at this high volume, but keep going forward I am with you. I know who you are, I know what you have been through. The more difficult the test, the greater My reward will be." The Lord told me that as I passed the testing of my faith that I was moving up in the ranks as a soldier in the army of the Lord God Almighty.

I said: "Amen!" "Please don't leave me!" The Lord promised, He would not. After about a half hour of hearing instructions and getting a full explaination of why I was having nightmares, the high volume voice faded, but the overwhelming joy of the Lord did not ever depart me. I was now officially on assignment for the Lord. Confirmed and full of joy that I had this confirmation. I was excited and anxious to tell my wife what had just happened to me. That was five months into my sabbatical.

Over breakfast I told my wife and she was blown away because she could see the overwhelming joy, peace, and glow that was on me. Her exact words were:" Wow! I wish that had happened to me". She told me how lucky I was to have a close encounter. I felt extremely happy and blessed. I definitely was not going to stop praying now. I knew that I had to start getting ready to come out of my prayer closet and start making my faith known to all men; that the merciful God is watching us closely. My testament is that Jesus Christ is alive and well, resurrected with all power and glory. Wanting no man to perish, but have everlasting life. God wants us to seek Him in spirit and in truth by praying, worshiping and trusting Him, especially when difficult times come our way. I was right on cue when quitting my job at the car dealership that day. I now know why I was tormented on December 14th, 2012. In the midst of being so out of touch with God, God really never left me even though I had left Him and became as average as any person can be whether thet have faith or not. I did the right thing by quitting my job that day and stepping out in faith. To trust God to change me from the inside out. God promised to bless me and this was only the beginning of the plans that He had for me. The revelation that He shared with me that morning was that I was a changed man no matter who or what was in front of me. He said that His blessing would continually change every area in my life for His glory. He left me with the impression that the blessing was not only for me, but for all believers that prayed and sought out to Him in spirit and in truth. What a powerful revelation! The core of true ministry.

A few days after that revelation I started campaigning hard for the Lord proclaiming the Kingdom of God. Now a days one of the best and fastest ways to share the Gospel is through social media networks online. My online friends must have thought that I lost my mind because whenever I would post something, I always put a sign on my wall that read. " Kingdom Time: Mind, Body, and Soul". I began to proclaim my faith to all who would hear me and share encouraging messages. I could not stop saying to myself: it's KINGDOM TIME, it has to been since the resurrection of Jesus Christ from His death on the cross for the world over two thousand years ago. The Kingdom of God and Heaven is here on earth. I accept that and want to always be part of it. I feel close to God's presence daily. That my motto everyday even as I am writing this book, I am reminded that "IT IS KINGDOM TIME, ALL THE TIME". Don't ever forget that. God is with the prayer warriors. The peace and the promise of God's Holy Spirit is for those that seek Him in spirit and in truth. You will find Him if you seek God. That is a promise that God alone will keep. I am a witness. Glory to God!

John 14:15-21King James Version (KJV)

15 If ye love me, keep my commandments.16 And
I will pray the Father, and he shall give you another
Comforter, that he may abide with you for ever;

17 Even the Spirit of truth; whom the world cannot receive, because it seeth him not, neither knoweth him: but ye know him; for he dwelleth with you, and shall be in you.

18 I will not leave you comfortless: I will come to you.

19 Yet a little while, and the world seeth me no more; but ye see me: because I live, ye shall live also.

20 At that day ye shall know that I am in my Father, and ye in me, and I in you.

21 He that hath my commandments, and keepeth them, he it is that loveth me: and he that loveth me shall be loved of my Father, and I will love him, and will manifest myself to him.

Prayer:

Father, bless my friends who are reading this right now. I pray that they would find faith in their heart to start seeking after you, for wisdom and guidance. I pray that as they put their faith in you, that you would bless them, forgive them of any and all sins and anoint their lives with the Holy Spirit as you have blessed me. May whomever is reading this prayer find their treasure and calling in life as a believer of the Gospel of the Lord Jesus Christ. You promised Lord to bless those who obeyed and followed you. Help them, Spirit of the true and living God to hear your voice and do your will. Give them strength to trust in you no matter what. In Jesus name Amen.

CHAPTER 11

TIME TO GET BACK TO THE HOUSE OF GOD

The encounter I had with the Holy Spirit was gifted to me after my personal sabbatical through prayer and fasting. I believe that God always wanted me to become a true intercessor for the community. Part of the vision I experienced on the day when God opened my eyes and ears was to return to the house of God to share my testimony and new found faith with my brothers and sisters. To encourage them, that no matter what, having faith in God is the pathway to fully restoring life when we seek Him. To encourage the church that Jesus is alive and the blessing of eternal life, power, and peace is within us. The blessing is beautiful, it is filled with power, and so holy that we must learn to take private prayer time and reverence to God almighty seriously. Why? So we can protect it and ourselves. The only person that can ruin and change the pathway to continued blessings is the believer. Due to a lack of faith and not doing what we know to be right in God's sight. We can no longer let others that are clueless to God's peace or purpose lead us astray. God does not wait until you finish college or gain titles in ministry before he decides to bless you. The Lord looks at what the average man does not see,which is the heart, the will, and the motivation behind every prayer that is lifted up in His name while praying in private.

On Easter Sunday I made it back to the house of God. The house where God originally gave me the kneeler idea to encourage prayer and where I fellowshipped often. I am committed to share the love of Christ with all people even those that failed me. To let them know God's love and forgiveness never runs out. It is my mission in life to live out this race of winning souls for Christ in His peace, regardless of who believes in the message that God gives me. If God blessed me with His holy anointing at my very own home, after leaving the church, and basically giving my back to everyone, how much more won't God bless his people who do attend church weekly! I believe in the church. That is where we learn about God, that is where pray for each other and stay encouraged in regards of who we are to God. I believe God loves all churches, but He especially loves a church that not only preaches the truth,but that also has faith in Christ to live in peace with all men no matter the cost.

So many of us give up too soon. We overwhelm ourselves when we are not properly prepared for evangelism because we may not understand the level of blessings that God is going to give us to complete His work. So we rush things instead of maintaining in His peace and maturing in Christ. We think that God has forgotten our efforts, but He has not. So we delay our blessings due to a lack of faith, real relationship, endurance, and character. Trials come, yes, but they are there for a reason. To build up our character in who we are in Christ. God is calling us to have more faith in Him during this time of purification. He knows the day and time we live in. He is not ignorant to what is going on in this world. He see's and knows every trap the enemy has set to bring His faithful ones down. We must not give up. The churches now a day need a fresh revelation. To stay real with one another, care for one another with pure hearts and motives. Never forgetting that the day of the Lord's return is near. We don't need to scare anyone into becoming a Christian by forcing them to pray or even follow us. What we need to do is shine our light on the world, forgiving those that offend us, learning how to love people for who they are regardless of their shortcomings. That is how you win people over for God and at the same time stay protected, by praying for the lost and having a heart of hope and understanding for the hurting. In turn God blesses you. Daily God gives real revelations on the treasures of His Kingdom. The peace and blessing of acknowledging God and an eternal Kingdom is incredible. It will change your life once you dedicate your life to living for God according to His word.

The freedom that I live in Christ, is worth me singing about because it gives me much peace to know that with the Lord by my side I am safe no matter where I am, whether I am at church, the gym, work, or on a recreational outing with my family. I always knew that, but somewhere along my journey of faith, I got lost and kept the Lord out of things that I enjoyed. I kept Him out of things I knew I needed to include Him in, sometimes at the hands of others that made me feel lesser. Deep down I always knew that I was more than blessed to enjoy the fruit of my labor. The work I did for the Lord with the prayer pillows is no longer in my hands. It never was, and at the end of the day, I did not fail God and God certainly did not fail me. Man failed to connect in faith with me during my building process only seeing what they wanted to see. But I learned to forgive and move on. God reminds me to maintain in His peace at all times. The burden has been lifted. The overwhelming peace and strength of God is what I live for now that I have truly found it. The Holy Spirit is directing God's people to things that give us peace and motivation to live life. We can now joyfully advance the Kingdom of God anywhere because we are free in Christ. We are free from judgement. We are free from man. We are strong in the Lord who always fights for our liberty which is found in faith through Christ. We aught to pray and seek to know who God really is. Don't get left behind by failing to learn who God is. Seek Him. The blessing is real and through fervent bible study, prayer, and obedience the blessing is found and kept protected.

Trials come and go but the victorious ones are the ones who run this race with passion. God has called some people out of some very dark and lonely places to help the weak in faith stay the course. Now that they have found their strength in Christ. I could have chosen to listen to that voice that said, "who cares" on December 14, 2012. I am so glad I did not. I am so glad I had faith and was able to repent and able to come back home to a heavenly father that cares. In the midst of so much disappointment with people inside and outside of the church, I decided not to give up on the church either. I finally realized that my real strength does not come from church folk. The strength we all long for comes from having a real personal relationship with God almighty through prayer. And He speaks to whoever will listen. Most of the messages that God gives me are to never give up on myself. This faith walk is about staying motivated, lovable, and purpose driven. We must take care of our bodies (which is the temple of God) through exercise and nutrition. Always setting positive goals confidently knowing that he will help the believer achieve them. He constantly reminds me that He is there for all who trust in Him. I know that the voice that I hear is of God, because it is always followed by a great blessing of peace when I take the time to obey His lead.

Having a relationship with God is what makes life worth living. We have to put our faith in Him and it does require work at times, but he does the work through us if we let Him. He shall reward each believer accordingly. He is our healer. He is no respecter of persons, meaning that God can and will use anyone to establish His kingdom here on earth. No matter how many times trials come, don't let the trial keep you from God. Pray through it! moving forward in what God has called you to do. Failure oftentimes is part of the process of achieving success somewhere down the road. Trusting God's word will help the believer refrain from becoming bitter should success not come in a timely manner. Have faith, it will arrive. There are no failures in God's people, only lessons learned to help us all stay the course. Use your failures to help others not make the same mistake, all of your experiences good or bad are valuable in the hands of the almighty God. Roman 8:28

Once you start moving in faith and doing the will of God, (shedding light and compassion to all) your life will be full of the internal and external blessings because now you are doing your part to be the best citizen in God's kingdom. Knowing that alone is very fulfulling because no one ever likes to feel overwhelmed or feel like they are not doing enough to please the Father. God does not overwhelm His children to the point of anyone wanting to give up totally. If you are a runner in God's race, pace yourself like a marathon runner and train daily (pray, worship, study, give) in this race because it is going to take endurance, rest and daily strength to achieve being the best person you have ever wanted to be. When you pace yourself and come up with your customized goals stay faithful and live life. That pleases God. He wants you to be at your best all the time. God is peace, God is wisdom, God is power, God is grace, God is love, God wants the overcomer to come alive and be His heavenly image here on earth. Shining your light over darkness now that we have been redeemed from this world of sin and confusion.

God has taken this sick, injured man and has transformed his life. God has healed me so now I can have healthy relationships. God is not doing it for me because I invented a unique prayer pillow. God is doing it because I continue to seek Him daily. I exercise my mind, body, and soul in total reverence to Him daily. I should have given up. The world hurt me by it being so cold and heartless concerning the things of God. The church (not all churches) hurt me by being so unbelieving to the revelation that God was with me when He told me to make prayer pillows and encourage people to pray reverently in private.

I refuse to die another day to someone else's unbelief in me or God. If the prayer pillow/encouragement is not for you then it is not for you, but God knows I have always had my brothers and sisters in Christ best interest. I know the calling I have is from God to encourage prayer to encourage people to stay humble and real as success comes our way. We have an enemy though that likes to make believers who are creative feel bad, like we are never doing enough when we get to certain levels in this walk, when in reality it is them (the accuser) that is not doing their part to uplift and embrace vision. We silence that enemy through our fervent prayers to God almighty. Don't listen to negative or fear-filled voices unless you have prayed fervently about it, because it is always God that give us the strength to get things done. The struggles and judgement we sometimes face by others are won on our knees proving always to God almighty that we have pure thoughts and motives behind anything we do or say.

In the bible Paul tells us that the weapons of our warfare are not carnal, 2 Corinthians 10:4. We do not fight off negativity or worldliness with man made weapons or bad behavior. We fight the enemy off by the word of God, by the pulling down of strongholds casting down every thought that would make us higher than God in our own minds. 2 Corinthans 10:5. Many times we fail in our goals or projects because we begin to lose focus on who we are in Christ. Jesus always walked humbly and in much wisdom and power. Staying humble and walking with humility is not weakness because at the end of the day, we all need each other. The bible says be wise in all things. Peaceful solutions is a gift from God. Matthew 5:9

Sometimes we let pride come in and whether it be worldly or spiritual pride (highmindedness) pride is pride. That is why we must make prayer and reverence to God Almighty a priority. We should always remember that we are always being watched from heaven from the one who sits on the high throne and judges us correctly. His judgement toward us is so correct that if we are listening to God with our hearts it should lead us to conviction which leads us to repentance. It is our choice to repent or not. The wise person should choose to repent and forsake the weight of sin because repentance from errors always leads to a blessed life. God is the righteous judge of all matters, who blesses us according to His word.(Matthew 5:45) Any heavenly rewards that do not manifest on earth will always manifest itself in heaven and as a believer you are now a Citizen of Heaven. Whether the blessing was designed to manifest itself in this life or the next life to come. Hold on to the promise. No matter what, hold on to your faith in God because you will recieve that crown of blessings one day. That's faith eternal, that leads to life eternal. Matthew 6:20

As man streches the limits in society to see what is acceptable to God to reach His eternal heaven. Let us that live in truth going to God's word, spending quality time in prayer with God alone so he can lead us and guide us because if we are studying God's word correctly the presence of God will show up, leading us to fellowship with like minded believers.

God's love is unconditional and He wants to bless His children with His peace. If you are living your life with guilt after you have prayed and asked for forgiveness and still feel depressed, that is not the spirit of the Lord. Keep praying and keep believing. God's love covered all sin, future struggles and shortcomings at the cross. There is no sin in this world that God can not forgive. God knows the environment that we are growing up in. We still have time to recieve His love and get that new perspective on life that God has always wanted for us since the beginning of time. He is able to keep us from ever falling or sinning again.

24 Now unto him that is able to keep you from falling, and to present you faultless before the presence of his glory with exceeding joy, Jude 1:24 King James version

God's purpose for our life will always have meaning. We just need to seek Him and obey the Spirit of the Lord that lives in us after we have committed our ways to Him. The Holy Spirit is real and that tug in our hearts to repent, to pray, or to worship God is there to help us stay the course to His blessings. Don't fight it, just surrender your life to God and have faith that God is on your side. We perfect our walk in God, hour by hour, day by day, one day at a time.

2 Beloved, I wish above all things that thou mayest prosper and be in health, even as thy soul prospereth. 3 John 1:2 King James Version

I can not say this enough, God gives strength to those that honor and reverence Him. Your life will gracefully evolve into becoming someone great, if you begin taking those baby steps of faith to becoming all you can for the glory of God. You don't have to stay a baby in your faith forever. God wants to mold you into a peaceful, joyful, fair, understanding, righteous king or queen for His kingdom even if the kingdom is only being manifested in your home, so what, be all that you can be for God. Don't let the world mold you into becoming somebody incomplete. Jesus completed the work on the cross that some might become a citizens of Heaven. Not tomorrow, but today! Yes today! The call is made from heaven everyday like a Facebook post. Don't give up, have faith, God is for you and with you.

It's always ok to take time to pray and humble yourself before the Lord. And even though the laws are changing concerning prayer in schools there will never be a law in your home that says you can not pray. I prefer praying in private as the scriptures say so that when I do pray in secret God will reward me openly. There is a mighty church of believers that will not stop praying and believing God's word until they get to the promised land. It's time to believe that God, the real father of Jesus Christ is the rewarder of those that diligently seek him (Hebrew 11:6) more than ever before! Do not lose any more faith, go for your best life now. The presence that you feel after you have believed God's word, prayed, or worshipped God almighty whether at church or home that fills your heart with hope and joy, that is the Kingdom, run on that. If you don't feel anything at first, that's ok too, just keep praying and having faith and learning who God is. Little by little you are growing. God has promised in His word to never leave those that believe in Him, nor forsake those that believe in Him.

Jesus said: "just a little faith can move a mountain" (Matthew 17:20), work hard, love God, love people and enjoy each day with confidence. God will always bless you if you share your light and lead those that are straying off course or hurting back to the Lord.

In closing I just want to take time to thank you for reading my testimony. If you have been encouraged to keep going forward by my testimony. Please forward a copy of this book to any friend that needs a word of encouragement. I also encourage you to try a Kingdom Time Kneeler.

The kneeler/prayer pillow has been such a blessing to my life to help me pray in comfort reverently. Some spiritual breakthoughs would not have occured in my life, had I not humbled myself and prayed in this manner. Thankfully now because I no longer fear knee pain I can pray and praise God reverently in comfort. I have gotten many breakthoughs and revelations because I was able to pray a little longer without fearing knee pain. Had it not been for my strong prayer life I don't know where I would be. The anointing of God's Holy Spirit is real and always available. He gives you the blessed power and peace to dream and pursue all your goals. Jesus said: "Therefore I say to you, whatever things you ask when you pray, believe that you receive them, and you will have them." Mark 11:24

Beloved, I wish above all things that thou mayest prosper and be in health, even as thy soul prospereth. 3 John 2:1

Running towards the Kingdom, is the acknowledgement that there is more ahead of us in God if we keep the faith. Mind, Body, and Soul. May the blessing of the Lord Jesus Christ always be with the believer and every prayer answered speedily. Amen

Printed in the United States
By Bookmasters